Edinburgh and Lothians

Exploring the Lost
Railways

Other books by the author:

Published by GC Books Ltd
The Lost Railway Lines of Galloway
The Lost Railway L:ines of Ayrshire
Lost Railway Lines South of Glasgow

Published by Stenlake Publishing Ltd
Borders Railway Rambles

Cover photographs:
front : 'Granton Station, circa 1950' (Hamish Stevenson collection)
back (left): Tynehead looking north, (collection of the late Cecil J B Sanderson);
Glencorse, looking to Edinburgh, 18.5.63 (Hamish Stevenson collection)

Edinburgh and Lothians

Exploring the Lost
Railways

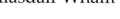
65334 on square crossing at Bonnington

Alasdair Wham

G C Books Ltd, Wigtown

For Murray and Morag

Acknowledgements

My thanks are due to my son Scott for his companionship on the journeys and for production of the maps; to my wife Christine for her continued support; to David Tough for his considerable help and support in editing the text and for his many constructive comments; to Hamish Stevenson for contributing the railway photographs taken by him and his father and for access to his photographic collection; to Beverley Chadband (GC Books Ltd) for all her help and support and to Mike Clayton for considerable help with the layout and design.

I also gratefully acknowledge the following for permitting the use of photographs from their collections :   the late Cecil J B Sanderson 'Tynehead looking north' - back cover; 'Gorebridge Station looking north', p53; the late Graham E Langmuir (Mitchell Library, Glasgow) 'Glencorse Viaduct', p80; the late J F McEwan (William Patrick Library) 'Scotland Street looking to northern portal' p95; K M Falconer 'Haddington Station' p21; W S Sellar '65334 on Square Crossing at Bonnington', title page, 'Site of House O'Hill' p108. Remaining photographs from Hamish Stevenson's collection.

ISBN 9781872350141
(1872350143)

Published by:
G C Books Ltd,
Unit 10 Bladnoch Bridge Estate,
Bladnoch,
Wigtown.
DG8 9AB
email: gcbooks@btinternet.com

Contents

Maps

Abbreviations

CR	Caledonian Railway
EBR	Edinburgh and Bathgate Railway
ECML	East Coast Main Line
EDR	Edinburgh and Dalkeith Railway
EGR	Edinburgh and Glasgow Railway
ELGR	Edinburgh, Leith and Granton Railway
ELRR	Edinburgh, Loanhead and Roslin Railway
ENR	Edinburgh and Northern Railway
EPDR	Edinburgh, Perth and Dundee Railway
EVR	Esk Valley Railway
LMSR	London, Midland and Scottish Railway
LNER	London North Eastern Railway
MKR	Monklands and Kirkintilloch Railway
MR	Monklands Railway
NBR	North British Railway
NER	North Eastern Railway
PR	Peebles Railway
PkR	Penicuik Railway
SBR	Slamannan and Borrowstounness Railway
SR	Slamannan Railway
WMCR	Wilsontown, Morningside and Coltness Railway

Introduction

The custodian of the Scott Monument in Edinburgh shows great confidence in every visitor. Once your admission fee is paid, a certificate is issued to certify that you have managed to climb the 287 steps to the top of the 200 foot monument - all you have to do is fill in your name. Don't cheat; the climb is worthwhile. This Gothic challenge completed in 1844 as a memorial to Sir Walter Scott, the famous Scottish writer, towers over Princes Street and rewards the effort required to climb it with increasing panoramic views over Edinburgh and further afield.

The view in any direction from the Scott Monument is both historical and interesting. Immediately to the south across the narrow valley which once contained the now drained Nor' Loch is the start of the Royal Mile and the Old Town and slightly west, the magnificent Edinburgh Castle perched on Castle Rock. To the north is Calton Hill and the grandeur of the Georgian New Town with views over the Firth of Forth to the Kingdom of Fife. This is tourist Edinburgh with visitors flocking to Princes Street and the many sights and sounds of this vibrant city especially around the world-famous Edinburgh Festival held in August each year.

To those interested in the history of railways, the view from the monument shows the challenges the railway builders faced in constructing the network of tracks that developed in and around the city. The arrival of the railway, in 1846, in the historic centre of Edinburgh was controversial and opposition only mollified by containing the railway in a cutting and restricting the height of railway buildings. Cramped between the Castle Rock and Princes Street and with its centre lying between Waverley Bridge to the west and North Bridge to the east is Waverley Station – the beating heart of Lothian's railways. The site was originally occupied by three stations, all initially belonging to different railway Companies, when first the North British Railway (NBR) and then the Edinburgh and Glasgow Railway (EGR), taken over by the North British in 1865, both terminated near North Bridge. The third station on the site, Canal Street, opened in 1847 and, operated by the Edinburgh, Leith and Granton Railway Company (ELGR), was at right angles to the first two and gave access to the Scotland Street tunnel. The site underwent several name and structural changes but by the 1860's it was known as Edinburgh Waverley. The station's name is linked with Sir Walter Scott and his series of famous Waverley novels, so it is fitting that his monument towers over the station.

The station site evolved, expanding east and west, but struggled to cope with increases in traffic. Successive improvements were soon negated by additional branches feeding into the station. When the railway bridge over the Forth opened in 1890, the North British began a complete reconstruction of the station which even required altering the North Bridge. The Scott Monument provides an overview of the station site and its extensive ridge and furrow glass canopy. The opening, in 1902, of the imposing North British Hotel designed by Sir William Hamilton Beattie and now known as the Balmoral, completed the redevelopment. Even after reconstruction, the station has no imposing facade to draw attention to it, with all passengers having to descend to reach the platforms. When it was opened, the only British station with more platform area was London's Waterloo Station.

To the west, the railway enters a 130 yard tunnel beneath the Royal Scottish Academy and the National Gallery of Scotland on the Mound, emerging briefly

Waverley Station from Scott Monument

before entering the longer 1040 yard Haymarket tunnel which passes under Lothian Road. Early opposition from the Bank of Scotland, whose headquarters are on the Mound, forced the railway to remain out of sight so as not to block their view. At the western end of Princes Street is the four-storey red sandstone Caledonian Hilton on Lothian Road, once part of the Caledonian Railway's Princes Street Station, opened in 1903, and built to rival the North British hotel at the other end of Princes Street. Prestige for railway companies has always been important. The station closed in 1965.

The Caledonian Railway's branch from Carstairs Junction reached Edinburgh in 1848 but was initially beset by the Company's financial problems at that time. One consequence was that the terminus at Lothian Road was wooden for a long time and described by the embarrassed railway company as 'temporary'. In 1869, the Caledonian built a shorter route via Cleland in Lanarkshire to increase competition on the important inter-city route between Glasgow and Edinburgh. The attractive Balerno branch which served the many mills along the Water of Leith left this inter city route near Slateford.

East from Waverley Station, the tracks pass under North Bridge. The problem for the railway builders in Edinburgh was that to the north of Waverley Station is the high ground occupied by the Georgian New Town and Calton Hill. To the railway builders, this was a major obstacle to reaching the ferries which crossed the Firth of Forth towards Fife before the Forth Railway Bridge was opened. The first solution was to tunnel under the New Town to reach Scotland Street before continuing the journey to the coast at Granton, Newhaven and Leith but the gradients meant that the carriages had to be hauled by cable through the tunnel and the railway was never successful. Although the tunnel closed in 1868, it still exists with one recent suggestion that it could become an underground shopping mall.

The only way to the ports involved a detour around the high ground and the North British route was forced east of the New Town and Calton Hill before eventually branching from their Berwick line to reach the ports at Leith, Newhaven and Granton. The Caledonian Railway (CR) arrived on the scene later and skirted the high ground of the New Town to the west to reach first Granton and then Leith. The scramble to service the ports on the coast led to a dense network of lines and stations but the detours forced on the railways put them at a disadvantage with the buses which could take more direct routes.

In 1831, the first Edinburgh railway opened but it did not run through the centre of Edinburgh. It started at St Leonards Depot beside Salisbury Crags, near Arthur's Seat about a mile from the castle. The Edinburgh and Dalkeith Railway (EDR) initially descended on a steep gradient, requiring cable haulage, through St Leonards tunnel, cut through a spur of rock protruding from Salisbury Crags and headed towards the Lothian coalfield to the south. Coal, not passengers was the initial attraction. This network, based on horse-drawn wagons, expanded towards Leith and Fisherrow near Musselburgh but only lasted fourteen years before the emergence of the NBR.

That company took over the Edinburgh and Dalkeith in 1845 and by 1847 had modified and expanded the network. The Waverley Route south of Edinburgh branched at Portobello, using parts of the EDR before heading south through Midlothian and the Scottish Borders to reach Hawick. It was extended over Whitrope Summit to Carlisle in 1862 thus creating a third Anglo-Scottish Route. Branching from the Waverley Route, railway engineers must have cursed the deep valleys gouged by the Rivers North and South Esk which they frequently had to cross. Sensibly, the North British allowed private companies to construct the routes before taking them over. The lure of the coal deposits of the Lothian coalfields and the profits generated by them, encouraged the opening of branches to Penicuik, Polton and the loop to Peebles which rejoined the Waverley Route near Galashiels. Passenger services were also important and if the branches were still open today, they would have enlarged the commuter belt around Edinburgh and reduced congestion on the roads. Closed in 1969, the partial re-opening of the Waverley Route to Tweedbank, south of Galashiels, will hopefully rejuvenate both Midlothian and the Borders and allow them to join in Edinburgh's economic growth. Stations have already opened at Brunstane and Newcraighall.

The North British route, which originally terminated at Berwick and is now part of the East Coast Main Line, allowed the development of branches to Musselburgh and Smeaton with access to Macmerry and Gifford, Haddington, Aberlady and Gullane, and North Berwick. All those lines served East Lothian with only the North Berwick branch now surviving. The volume of coal traffic from the mines around Dalkeith and the East Lothian pits created a bottleneck at Portobello which led to the construction of the 'Lothian Lines' to ease access to the harbour at Leith.

In Edinburgh, with the support of the North British, the Edinburgh, Suburban and Southside Junction Railway known as the 'Sub' opened in 1884. It branched from the Waverley Route, looping to the south of the Old Town and passing through Newington and Craiglockhart before rejoining the intercity route west of Haymarket near Gorgie. The route also relieved the pressure on the busy main line through Waverley Station especially for freight. An even later North British addition to the rail network was the short branch to Leith Central only seven minutes from Waverley via Abbeyhill or twenty-one minutes from Morningside by the south suburban route. Probably the biggest new build station in Britain in the twentieth century, Leith Central opened in 1903 with its grand proportions amazing everyone. The station was built partly to block Caledonian plans to create an underground route from Leith to Princes Street and, at least in that, it was successful. The station lost out to the trams and closed within fifty years; a monument to the folly of too much competition.

Returning to the view from the monument, prominent on the horizon to the west is Corstorphine Hill where the world famous Edinburgh Zoo is located. The main line towards Glasgow and the north passed to the south of Corstorphine Hill but the Caledonian branch to Barnton curved to the north, branching from the route to Granton at Craigleith. The short North British branch to Corstorphine left the main line to the south of the hill. Beyond Corstorphine Hill, the cantilever Forth Railway Bridge can be seen beside the Forth Road Bridge; world class iconic engineering constructions. The railway bridge provided the important missing railway link to the north. The opening of the bridge also reduced the importance of the NBR route from Ratho to Queensferry which took passengers and freight to the ferry services around Queensferry.

The railways of West Lothian which were traversed by the inter city routes of both the North British and Caledonian Railways can't be seen from the Scott Monument but there is a link to the county; the sandstone from which the monument is constructed was quarried there. The inter city routes between Glasgow and Edinburgh, built by the Edinburgh and Glasgow and Caledonian Railways, both survive but much of the railway network in West Lothian, built on traffic from oil shale and coal production, has disappeared although the branch to Bathgate was re-opened and speculation increases that the railway from Bathgate to Airdrie (at present a cycle route) will also re-open.

With an increasing population and gridlock on many roads, the story of the Edinburgh and Lothian railway network is not yet complete. With admirable foresight, sections of the disused railway network have been preserved and are worth investigating. This book explores the many disused railway routes in the Lothians and the railway heritage left by the railway builders. That so much remains after the last train has departed, is a tribute to the railway engineers.

Exploring the Railway Heritage

A surprising amount of railway heritage remains in the Lothians and hopefully this book will help you to both recognise and appreciate it.

The following points are intended to encourage responsible exploration.

1. Please do not assume that because a journey or place is described in this book that you have permission to follow in my footsteps. This book is not intended as a book of walks. Unless a route has been recognised as an official walkway then the fact that I have been able to follow most of the routes is not meant to imply that a right of way exists or that they are suitable for walking. Fortunately, many of the walks in the area are recognised cyclepaths.

2. If you do intend to trace any part of a route, where possible, seek permission from the landowner who will probably be pleased to let you walk the trackbed. Being a responsible explorer will promote goodwill and allow others to follow in your footsteps. Seek permission where possible and respect the Country Code. Access will always depend on courtesy and mutual trust.

3. Many former station buildings are now private residences and while owners are usually pleased to talk about the history of their properties, there is no right of access. No-one wants a walker in their back garden.

4. Always keep away from dangerous structures. Most of the viaducts, bridges and tunnels have not been maintained for over thirty years, some a lot longer. Do not cross fences or barriers erected for your safety.

5. Conditions on the routes change all the time. When I first explored the branch from Ormiston to Gifford the station master's house at Pencaitland Station still stood. On a recent visit it had been demolished. Over time, similar changes are likely to occur particularly in urban areas.

6. If possible, check out a route beforehand especially in country areas and be prepared for unexpected detours. All distances given are approximate. A missing bridge can result in a lengthy detour. Use an up-to-date map. I have found the Ordnance Survey Explorer series to be the most useful.

7. Be aware of the weather. In Scotland it can change very quickly. Be equipped and in the more remote sections, check the bus times carefully or arrange for someone to pick you up.

The scenery in the Lothians is superb and there is plenty for historians, industrial archaeologists, those with memories of the railway era or simply for the curious to enjoy.

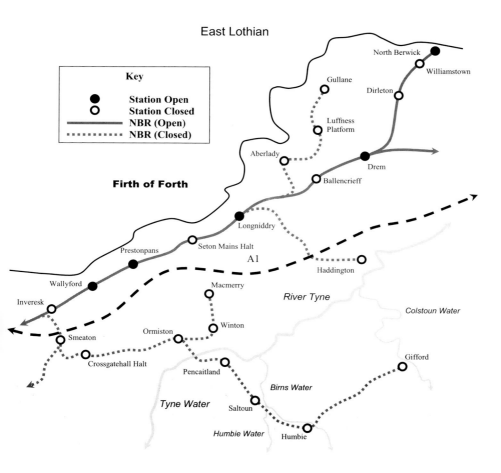

Chapter 1

Coal, Golf and Whisky:
The Abandoned Railways of East Lothian

The coastal plain between the Lammermuir Hills and the Firth of Forth contains some of the richest agricultural lands in Scotland. At the coast around Gullane and North Berwick are the sand dunes and beaches familiar to those who enjoy a day at the seaside or a game of golf. Near the western edge of East Lothian around Musselburgh and Tranent, the outcrops of the Lothian coalfields have been exhausted with the scars of the once important coal industry beginning to heal. One of the major arterial railway routes in Britain : the East Coast Main Line (ECML) from London to Edinburgh, bisects this countryside and a series of local railways branched from it to serve the varied communities of East Lothian.

In a curious way, this railway network reflected the many different land types and needs in East Lothian. The first branch to open was to the county town of Haddington, allowing people to commute between Haddington and Edinburgh but which also carried the agricultural produce of the fertile East Lothian farmlands to the city markets. Then followed the seaside resort lines, first to North Berwick and much later, Aberlady and Gullane, which took generations of people to the seaside and the famous East Lothian coastal golf links. The route from Smeaton to Ormiston was industrial and collected coal from the many pits along its way. At Ormiston, the line branched to Macmerry, another coal collecting route and to Gifford a quiet country town in the foothills of the Lammermuirs.

Today, only the North Berwick branch survives; the rest having been consigned to history with express trains on the ECML hurtling past closed and neglected junctions. Due to the foresight of the local council, two of the disused lines have survived as walkways - the Haddington branch and the Pencaitland Railway Walk which covers part of the Smeaton to Ormiston and Gifford lines. The Musselburgh branch which is also in East Lothian is covered in the chapter on the Waverley Route.

Haddington Branch

The Haddington line opened in 1846, branching from the North British Railway Company's Edinburgh to Berwick line at Longniddry Junction and climbing 200 feet to a summit near Merryhatton before dropping a hundred feet to reach Haddington, the historic and ancient county town of East Lothian. The twelve minute journey over the four and three quarter mile long route provided panoramic views over the Firth of Forth and north to the kingdom of Fife. Famous for the restored red sandstone Parish Church of St Mary, the town attracted attention from Christian pilgrims and became known as the Lamp of the Lothians. Haddington suffered from English invasions and the army of King Henry VIII laid siege to the town as part of the King's attempts to marry the infant Mary Queen of Scots to his son Prince Edward, a period of history which became known as the "rough wooing". The railway played a part in the history of the town for over a hundred years and has left its own legacy since the trackbed is now a railway walkway.

In 1970, the Scottish Railway Preservation Society showed serious interest in purchasing the line but reservations by some members over the viability of the proposals and a withdrawal of tenuous support from farmers, the people of Haddington and planning officers, proved fatal. The SRPS eventually acquired and restored the Boness and Kinneil Railway.

The North British Railway (NBR), who built and operated the branch, initially ran a scheduled service of five mixed passenger and freight trains each day with connections to Edinburgh and Berwick-upon-Tweed although not all trains made connections to both places. There was even a limited Sunday service consisting of two return trips which was surprising given the restrictions on Sabbath operation over later neighbouring routes such as the Aberlady and Gullane Branch. Although passenger numbers were initially disappointing, within two months of services starting, the North British were obliged to provide double track due to a threat which never materialised from the proposed East Lothian and Tyne Valley Railway. This route would have run from Dalkeith to Haddington by Ormiston and on to East Linton but it was never built and with the threat of a rival removed, the double track survived only ten years.

In spite of complaints about the standard of carriages during the NBR's ownership, by the turn of the century passenger numbers had increased to over seventy thousand annually with most travelling to Edinburgh but some using other local branches to reach the seaside. Eight trains a day were now timetabled. Passenger numbers fluctuated until 1925 after which they rapidly declined. Even the arrival of the nationalised British Railways in 1948 and a campaign of matching the price of bus fares was not enough to beat the competition from the roads.

With passenger numbers rising only marginally and the post-war railway having to conserve coal, the passenger service was withdrawn in December 1949 although the branch freight services continued until 1968.

The Friday grain market at Haddington was one of the most important in Britain and by 1850, a siding for grain traffic was provided at the station. Bermaline bread, produced in Haddington and exported all over the country created a lot of traffic for the line. The Haddington Gas Light Company imported coal although it did not have its own sidings and relied on horses for the journey from the station. Several local coal merchants also used the station yard. The livestock carried on the line was destined for local farms or the private Haddington Slaughterhouse Siding.

The Second World War brought increased traffic, due to an increased military presence, with troops based at Amisfield to the east and air force activity at Lennoxlove airfield to the south of the town. The First Polish Armoured Division, located at Amisfield, embarked at Haddington for the Normandy landings.

The Aberlady and Gullane Branch

Through the rich farmlands of East Lothian to the sandy beaches of Aberlady and Gullane Bays on the southern shores of the Firth of Forth, the short line which branched from the East Coast Main Line, one and a half miles east of Longniddry Station, passed through gentle rolling countryside. North Berwick Law provides a prominent landmark to the east, Cockenzie Power Station a less attractive landmark to the west while inland the Lammermuir hills frame the southern horizon. To the north, Fife is visible on a clear day. With no natural resources to exploit, this was not an industrial branch but a people's line. Indeed, for golf enthusiasts who enjoy the challenge of links golf, this was and still is paradise. The best of the world's golfers regularly rise to the challenge of the famous Muirfield Golf Course but there are also the Gullane Links and Luffness Links. The railway helped both golfers and holidaymakers to reach their destinations in the era before the bus or car.

Aberlady, once the busy port for Haddington before the arrival of the railway diverted business to that town, and Gullane, already prospering as a golfers' resort before the railway came, were the two main destinations. The arrival of the railway brought trainloads of holidaymakers and golfers to these towns and allowed them to share in the success of their larger neighbour, North Berwick which had experienced the benefits of a rail service for almost fifty years before the Gullane Railway finally opened in 1898. The breezes (and gales) from the

Forth could make a round of golf very challenging with conditions often changing hole-by-hole. The railway even opened a platform for the Luffness golfers who had, however, to inform the guard before the start of their journey if they wished to alight at the platform.

The official title of the railway was the Aberlady, Gullane and North Berwick Railway. The final section between Gullane and North Berwick, joining the existing track to North Berwick south of the town near Williamstown, was never constructed but this did not hinder the performance of the Aberlady and Gullane branch line. Its development followed a familiar pattern; promoted by local interest and quickly absorbed within two years by the NBR. Despite several attempts, the connection between Gullane and North Berwick never materialised. As late as 1915, the people of Gullane were petitioning the NBR to complete the link quoting reduction in the cost of running the railway and encouragement to build more houses as advantages. With eight golf courses in the area, there would have been no shortage of demand for those wishing to live beside the fairways.

Six trains ran between Longniddry and Gullane on weekdays with the journey taking thirteen minutes. There were extra trains on a Saturday between Aberlady and Gullane but no Sunday service. By the time of the takeover by the NBR, nearly fifteen thousand passengers a year were using Aberlady Station and over twenty thousand a year using the facilities at Gullane. The effect on the two communities was also marked, with the number of people living in Gullane more than doubling. Goods services were not successful with only one cattle train a week on Tuesdays. Aberlady Station attracted a gas works which survived successfully for many years. The line even boasted an express when in 1912, the North British introduced the Lothian Coast Express between Glasgow Queen Street and Dunbar with sections of the train going to Gullane and North Berwick. Modern carriages and new Scott class locomotives were used and the express was one of the first to serve food. It ran during the summer months, a peak time for business on the branch, and continued until 1932. The Lothian Coast Express was the first named train in the United Kingdom to feature its name on a locomotive headboard.

By 1930, passenger figures had dropped alarmingly due to competition from buses; Aberlady Station some distance to the south of the village was particularly vulnerable. The passenger service was withdrawn by the London North Eastern Railway (LNER) in 1932 although excursions and specials continued to run into the British Railways era. The route closed to all traffic in 1964.

Smeaton to Macmerry and Gifford

The scars of the past are still apparent around the site of Smeaton Station where the lines to Macmerry and Gifford start to cross the rolling East Lothian landscape. The railway branched from the ECML at Monktonhall Junction, a mile and a half to the north of Smeaton Junction. Coal bings are still scattered around, mute monuments to the miners. The views north across the Firth of Forth can add a touch of beauty on a clear day but the magnificent Carberry Towers and Queen Mary's Mount with their royal connections, surrounded by woods, must have seemed to generations of miners and railwaymen, to belong to another very different world.

The first section of the line from Smeaton to Ormiston was opened for goods in May 1867 and extended to Macmerry in the following year. An intermediate station at Winton on the Macmerry branch was opened in May 1872, the same year as a passenger service along this section was introduced. It was the turn of the century before the line was extended from Ormiston south to the village of Gifford in the foothills of the Lammermuirs and additional stations at Pencaitland, Saltoun and Humbie built. Business from the coal mines feeding into the lines was brisk, requiring the line from Monktonhall to Smeaton to be doubled in 1912. A halt at Crossgatehall, to the east of Smeaton Station, was opened in 1913 but was closed under war time economies before re-opening in 1919. Both the halt and Smeaton Station were closed to passengers in 1930 and for Crossgatehall this meant total closure since it never had a goods service.

Originally, the Gifford line was to be extended to Garvald, a village to the north-east of Gifford, and an Act of Parliament to build the Gifford and Garvald Light Railway was obtained in July 1891. The NBR wanted to operate the line only as far as Gifford but not finance it, whilst the directors of the original company wanted to retain control and continue the branch to Garvald and possibly beyond to the ECML. These diverse aims not only caused divisions within the Board of Directors of the fledgling railway company but led to disagreements between them and the NBR. Eventually, a further parliamentary bill in 1893 was required to modify the original route of the railway which had also been intended to pass between the villages of West and East Saltoun before reaching Gifford and was to the north of the route finally constructed between Ormiston and Gifford. The altered route was more demanding and expensive to build and was finally chosen due to a dispute between the principal landowners: Fletcher of Saltoun and the Marquis of Tweeddale, both of whom had been promoting the line and were at various times directors of the railway. The final route passed through more of the Marquis' land. Financing of the line was still a problem and it required the passing of the Light Railway Act, with its economies in costs and a further parliamentary act in 1898, to progress its construction. The line finally opened in 1901.

The extension to Garvald was surveyed but forgotten until 1920 when plans were revived with a proposed extension to the ECML to form a loop out of the Gifford branch. Increased competition from the roads meant that the proposals came to nothing. Passenger services to Gifford were stopped in 1933 and although goods services continued until the station closed completely in 1959, it was served by road after the line was washed away near Humbie Station in 1948. The lines were progressively closed up to 1965 when rail services east of Smeaton Station stopped completely.

Exploring the Railway Heritage

All the routes in this chapter are covered by the following maps; Landranger 66;   Explorer 345, 351

Haddington to Longniddry

A railway walk exists along the trackbed from near the site of the former Haddington Station to . The walk is 4.75 miles in length and may be accessed from either the Haddington or Longniddry end or from a car park and picnic area at the former Coatyburn Siding. In Haddington, the start of the walk is accessed by turning right off the West Road (B6471) at Alderston Road to reach a car park which is a few hundred yards west of the former station site beside the first overbridge on the route. At the Longniddry end, there is a car park for the Railway Walk just to the east of Longniddry Station along the B1377 which gives access to the walk. It can also be accessed through a gate in the fence beside the down platform of Longniddry Station.

Starting at the Haddington end, the station site (507740) is now an industrial yard but a platform and several buildings link the site to its railway past. The original station buildings consisted of a small two-storey stone building, the ground floor of which was the booking office, at right angles to the single platform. An engine shed, engine turntable and sidings completed the station. By the 1880s, the passenger facilities were inadequate and a much grander two-storey brick building was constructed further to the east with the original station building becoming the

Haddington Station - 2.3.68

stationmaster's house. Perched on a steep slope, the view from Station Road was of a grand two-storey brick building. The entrance hall projected from the centre of the building and a covered stairway, to the right of the entranceway, of which the upper half was glass, ran down to a wide semi-circular forecourt which in turn led through ornate stone gateposts topped by lamps. A large clock on the gable end facing the town was a landmark much missed by the locals when the main station buildings were demolished. Imposing villas extended along both sides of the road from the station towards Edinburgh, well placed for commuters.

In December 1937, during snowy conditions, a train crashed through the buffers

Ornate stone gatepost topped by a lamp at the former entrance of Haddington Station

at the station and ended up perched above the station entrance. If it had continued just a few more yards, then it would have tumbled some distance on to the road below. No-one was seriously injured but the accident did spoil a good safety record at the station. The extensive canopy over the platform collapsed as a result of the heavy rain which disrupted the Borders and Lothian in August 1948 and caused widespread damage to the railway network in the area. With extensive flooding locally, much of Haddington was under water.

The station site is now occupied by the unimaginatively named 'Station Yard Industrial Site'. The original booking office, occupied at present by Oxfam, still survives as does a long stretch of platform. To the west of the station were other sidings facing both eastward and westward forming a triangle. Today this area is wasteland but it is possible to follow a path, for a few hundred yards, towards the first overbridge at Alderston Road where a car park (501740) gives access to the start of the official railway walk. The trackbed passes under another original overbridge with wing walls and then two modern bridges which carry a bypass to the north of the town and the A1. Both bridges leave space for a double track line if the route were ever to reopen!

The railway walk now reaches open countryside and heads north-west through rich agricultural land. On a gentle rising gradient, the trackbed climbs out of the valley of the River Tyne with views back over Haddington towards the Lammermuir Hills. Immediately to the right is the Hopetoun Monument on Byres Hill, the most westerly of the Garleton Hills. The monument was built in memory of the British victory over Napoleon and is one of several such memorials around the country.

The next overbridge is approached through a cutting. In this cutting, at 300 feet, was the summit of the line. The skewed-arch sandstone overbridge takes a minor road towards Huntington. Merryhatton Cottages are to the right and Merryhatton Farm to the left with a track linking the farm to the disused railway.

The trackbed is now tree-lined and ahead can be seen Cockenzie Power Station. From here, the railway descended towards the ECML and on this section, four years after the railway opened, a train travelling towards Longniddry was derailed on a stretch of low embankment. A rail with insufficient support broke and caused the engine to rock from side to side before leaving the line and ending up in a turnip field. The third class carriage came off worst ending upside down in the field. As a result of the accident, extra sleepers were inserted to provide firmer support. North of the accident site at Laverocklaw was the first of two sidings on the line. This siding which was mainly used for sugar beet and potatoes served Laverocklaw Farm to the west of the line and was finally closed about 1960. The siding had been lifted in July 1874 with the proviso that at one month's notice by the landowner it would be re-laid and, indeed, in October of the following year the siding had to be restored at the landowner's request.

The trackbed crosses the Coaty Burn and continues to descend towards the main line. Half a mile after the Laverocklaw siding, Coatyburn siding (468759) is reached. The siding survived until 1964 and served the farms at Coates to the east and Setonhill to the west. Iron ore from the nearby Garelton Hills was loaded here for many years. A picnic site located on the old loading bay is provided with a car park just before a reconstructed bridge over a minor road. Coatyburn narrowly missed being destroyed in the Second World War when a landmine exploded slightly to the west of the siding beside the road.

From the Coatyburn siding, the trackbed curves north-west towards the ECML. The overhead gantries of the electrified ECML become more apparent as Longniddry approaches. There are extensive views over the Forth to Fife and other landmarks such as North Berwick Law. Closer and to the right can be seen the remains of Redhouse Castle derelict since 1746 when the owner backed the wrong side in the Jacobite uprising and subsequently lost control. Further east but not easy to spot is the start of the Aberlady branch.

The walk runs parallel to the ECML for a quarter of a mile before reaching Longniddry Station (446763). The station is still open but is much changed and simplified. The goods shed and sidings are gone as is the island platform, the departure point for the Haddington branch from 1898. The island platform had been added when the Aberlady and Gullane branch opened.

There was one spectacular accident at Longniddry in December 1953 when a Royal Mail train hit an obstruction on the line at the station overturning the engine which landed beside the road (A198). The carriage as well as the tender and engine were badly damaged and the fireman died later of the injuries he sustained in the crash. Several others were also injured. The obstruction, a metal object, had fallen off a wagon attached to an earlier train. The embankment had to be re-inforced and the small blue brick retaining wall remains today.

Next to the station were three sidings. The Balwearie siding was located to the east of the station as were the Harelaw Limekilns sidings which veered from the ECML just before the Haddington branch. Opened in 1847 and located several hundred yards to the west of the station were the Longniddry Manure Sidings. Wasting nothing, horse dung scooped from the streets of Edinburgh and Leith, was sent here by rail and left to rot to produce a source of manure for local farmers.

Modern conservationists could learn a lot from this exercise in re-cycling which also raised funds for the local police. The siding was known locally as the 'Police Manure'. A private house, presumably with the biggest vegetables in the area, now occupies this site.

The Longniddry end of the branch has the reduced role of serving the ECML and providing a stop for the North Berwick branch. The station has been transformed with the two platforms altered to accommodate electrification and a

23

new footbridge. The town of Longniddry has grown considerably. The eastern edge is still restricted by the Gosford House Estate but the town has developed westwards as far as the Canty Burn and has extended towards the Seton Sands where a golf course prevents further expansion.

Aberlady Junction with 'Sunday Brig' in distance - 1955

Aberlady Junction to Gullane

Sadly most of the route of the Aberlady and Gullane branch has been returned to agricultural use and only small stretches can be traced. From Aberlady Junction to Aberlady, access is difficult and the route is probably better observed from the nearby A6137. Only the final stretch from the overbridge at Harry's Plantation on the Luffness to West Fenton Road to the outskirts of Gullane remains walkable. There were stations at Aberlady (1.4 miles from Aberlady Junction), Luffness Platform (3.2 miles from Aberlady Junction) and Gullane (4.8 miles from Aberlady Junction).

The Aberlady and Gullane Branch ran alongside the ECML for a quarter of a mile before turning north towards Aberlady. The signal box, now demolished, which controlled the junction (471773) was located in a cutting beside the road bridge known as the Spittal bridge which carried the B1377 Longniddry to Drem Road. A short distance on was the Sunday Brig built to help worshippers attend the parish church at Aberlady. Rebuilt in the 1920's, the bridge was demolished in 1989.

As the disused trackbed curves north towards Aberlady Station, it does so on a gently falling embankment. Surrounded in summer by fields of crops, the trackbed is used as an access road for Ballencrieff Mains Farm. Eventually the trackbed disappears, ploughed into local fields. Aberlady Station (471793) is located beside a road bridge, on the A6137, over the former branch. A long curving platform is located to the west of the road. A bungalow has replaced the station buildings and a caravan park known as 'The Sidings' occupies the site. The main station building was a long single-storey hip-roofed wooden structure with two chimneys. To the south, the field is used to grow turf for transplanting and some famous football grounds have been supplied. The concrete platform built on a brick base allowed

Aberlady Station with a visiting rail tour shown on 11.6.60

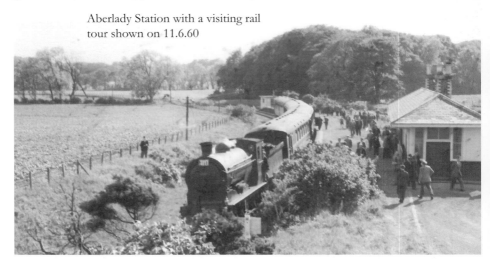

trains with many carriages to stop. There was, however, still quite a walk to the village itself. The station was one of those remote locations favoured by the Royal family and the Royal train was often to be found beside the station since it gave easy access to the ECML.

The Royal connection helps to explain why for many years after its closure, the station buildings were kept in pristine condition but another reason was that the station buildings were used until the 1960's as holiday accommodation for up to six persons in two bedrooms. To the other side of the road bridge, the trackbed is given over to agriculture. A detour is again required, taking first right and following the road towards Luffness Mains Farm. To the south of the road in Maggie's Waas Wood, there are traces of the trackbed and on the minor road to the motor museum at Myreton, south of Luffness Mains Farm, there is still a road bridge over the former trackbed. At the farm, the road turns sharp north and taking the first right along the Luffness to West Fenton road, the trackbed can be located at an overbridge just north of Harry's Plantation built to avoid a level-crossing.

An alternative route is to take the A6137 and then the Gullane Road. This passes through the village of Aberlady and around the now heavily silted Aberlady Bay where the Peffer Burn reaches the sea. The Aberlady Bay Nature Reserve covers the Gullane Sands and is popular with walkers. From the road bridge, bridge number 5, the former trackbed can be traced into Gullane. Lined by hedgerows, the trackbed quickly enters Peffer Bank Wood before crossing the Peffer Burn by another bridge, bridge number 6. The close proximity to Gullane means that the route is frequently used by dog walkers.

Luffness golfers' platform

Beyond the bridge over the Peffer Burn and just clear of the woods and to the left of the track, Luffness Platform was located. The wooden platform with a small hut halfway along was backed by a fence and was some distance from Luffness Golf Club House. On leaving the platform, the train passed the remains of Saltcoats Castle to the right of the line and Saltcoats Farm before entering Gullane itself. The castle dates from around 1530 and was inhabited until 1790.

The route is difficult to follow as it bypasses Gullane Primary School. A housing estate now occupies the station site (487829) and nothing remains of the

26

station building, engine shed, signal box, water tank or sidings. The road through the housing estate is known as 'Muirfield Station' which is slightly confusing. The station building was similar in construction to Aberlady station and, like that building, it was used as camping compartments and survived in good condition for many years. The station site fanned out in a vee-shape and is overlooked by the Scottish Fire Services College formerly the Marine Hotel. The eastern edge of the station site is now a fire station.

It was originally intended to extend the railway east of Gullane Station to meet the North Berwick line just south of that town. This line was never constructed but another railway, the two-foot gauge West Fenton Line, was built in 1915 to take building materials the one and a half miles from Gullane Station to the site of West Fenton airfield. The loading bay at Gullane was extended and the track built as simply as possible. The track turned sharply south when it reached the West Fenton Road and crossed the road at a level crossing north of the Mill Burn. Turning south again, it crossed the Mill Burn and a second level crossing took it over the road between West Fenton and Craighead Cottage before it reached the airfield.

The Aberlady and Gullane Branch had a short but busy life. Like many railways, it was doomed by the rise of the motor car and bus but is fondly remembered by generations of golfers and those who enjoyed a day at the seaside.

Smeaton Station to the start of the Pencaitland Railway Walk

The one mile section between Smeaton Junction, south of the station, and Crossgatehall Halt involved a steep climb for trains with the trackbed gaining a hundred feet. The trackbed is still traceable until the site of the level crossing near Smeaton Shaw farm. Beyond this point, the large bing at the former Dalkeith Colliery dominates the area obliterating most of the trackbed to the west of the road bridge where the A6124 and B6414 cross. On the Smeaton side of the road bridge was the site of Crossgatehall Halt, one mile from Smeaton Station. The halt was situated in a deep cutting known as the Cousland Gap which had to be cut through a high north to south ridge. A simple platform, with a waiting room and ticket office, was built to the north side of the track to placate the inhabitants of Cousland village, to the south-west of the halt, who felt bypassed by the railway. The station was more successful in attracting passengers than the other stations on the line to Macmerry. Nearby was a signal box which controlled access to the Dalkeith Colliery sidings and to the north of the cutting is the perimeter of the wooded grounds of Carberry Tower. The Cousland Gap has been largely filled in by the large bing previously mentioned.

Pencaitland Railway Walk - Start to Ormiston Station.

Access to the walk: The start of the six and a half mile Pencaitland Railway Walk is at Crossgatehall (370689) where a car park is provided. It is located a few hundred yards to the east of the road bridge over the trackbed where the A6124 and the B6414 cross. Boards provide information about the history of the railway although sadly these are prone to vandalism. There were no stations between Crossgatehall Halt and Ormiston Station (3.2 miles from Smeaton Station).

Eastward, the trackbed reaches its highest point between Smeaton and Ormiston at three hundred feet near the start of the railway walkway and drops about thirty feet by the time it reaches Ormiston. To the south, between the railway and the village of Cousland, were located the Cousland lime works and cement works. The lime from these works was used as plasterwork on the walls and ceilings in the houses of the New Town in Edinburgh. An earlier horse-drawn tramway to the cement works was replaced, in 1895, by a siding from which point a two-mile branch headed south-west to the long since closed Fordel Mains Colliery which extended almost to the A68.

The trackbed is surrounded by the gentle slopes of a valley running alongside the Bellyford Burn, a tributary of the Tyne Water, with the trackbed to the north of the burn. The scene is one of rural tranquillity with the only noises being the sound of contented animals munching and the buzz created by the overhead power lines sharing this sheltered valley. Sadly the burnt out wrecks of cars are also to be found. One wreck abandoned on this stretch contained the bodies of two murder victims but, thankfully, the victims along with their car have long since been removed!

Although the impression given by walking the trackbed today is of a quiet rural railway, this was not a sleepy rural line but a dirty noisy migration of clanking coal wagons edging westwards. On this stretch of the railway between Smeaton and Macmerry, there were at least fifteen sidings mostly leading to coal mines. It was an industrial artery pumping wagonloads of coal away from the pits to the cities, industrial sites around Scotland and to the Leith docks for export. Life for those who worked here was frequently difficult, demanding and dangerous but it was often the only means of earning a living. Workers, often children, crawled into the depths of the earth to scratch away at coal faces and drag heavy loads towards the surface where the coal was graded, sometimes washed, and sent down short mineral lines to join the main line. Now the area has been largely sanitised and ugly scars landscaped but it is important that the sacrifice of those who worked here is not forgotten. Appropriately, gravestone-sized memorials to different coal mines are found to the sides of the former railway giving a brief history of various local mines. After passing the remains of the branch to Fordell Mains Colliery, the trackbed passes through a tree-lined section with Elphinstone Tower to the north before reaching the site of the next siding to the north of the line which served Bellyford Pit. Following the closure of the pit, the siding was used by a farm and renamed Bellyford Siding. Almost on the opposite side of the railway was the original Cousland Siding which was replaced in 1895 by the siding of the same name further to the west.

Next, to the north, was a siding to another Bellyford Pit operated by R and J Durie of Tranent and a tramway to the Elphinstone Tower Pit. Oxenford Pit lay just to the south. Then followed a series of pits to the north starting at the Bog and Howden's Sidings and stretching along a mineral line that ended a mile north at Fleets Colliery which once employed over 800 men. During the Second World War, this was an award winning pit whose output easily exceeded its targets. Feeding in from the south was the output of the Limeylands, Tynemount and Oxenford Pits. Some sections of the disused trackbed which served these mines still exist to the west of Ormiston. Several coal bings are the only visible reminder of the output of these mines since the signal boxes which controlled access to the line and the many buildings at the various pitheads have all been removed.

Continuing eastward, the village of Ormiston with its prominent grain stores lies almost to the south and in the distance is the Hopetoun Monument on the summit of Byres Hill. The trackbed is crossed by a minor bridge as it approaches Ormiston Station which was dominated, between 1886 and 1909, by the Ormiston Station Colliery to the left. All that remains of the once busy station which closed for passengers in April 1933 is a platform ending at Puddle Bridge which carries the B6371 Ormiston to Tranent road over the former railway trackbed. The low station buildings and signal box have gone. A tall signal post which can provide a good viewing point for the station area was added when the railway was converted to a walk. Nowadays, the railway walk is accessed from a car park (415698) which is provided with picnic benches. Fruit was grown locally and at one time strawberries were sent by the first train from the station to Edinburgh to be enjoyed by royalty when in residence at Holyrood Palace.

The village is only a short distance from the former station and is worth a visit. A twenty-one foot tall granite obelisk commemorating the pioneering missionary work in South Africa of Dr Robert Moffat stands beside the road at the entrance to the village. His work inspired many, including David Livingstone, who married Moffat's daughter. John Cockburn (1685 to 1758), a pioneer of Scottish agriculture whose family owned the lands of Ormiston from 1368 to 1748 re-designed the village with its broad tree-lined streets and planted hedges in the surrounding countryside to enclose fields. The road bridge over the railway to the east of Ormiston Station has been strengthened because of subsidence. Beyond the bridge was Ormiston Junction where the railway branched with the line to Gifford turning sharply south and crossing the Puddle Burn after which the bridge was named and the branch to Macmerry turning north-east.

Ormiston Station to Macmerry

The first section of the route is now a minor road. This closely follows the former railway until a point near the B6355. The trackbed then cuts sharply north-east crossing what is now a farmer's field. The minor road, however, continues until the B6355 is reached. Turning left on to the B6355 and continuing to the abutments of the railway bridge, the trackbed can be rediscovered beside Winton Station (5.4 miles from Smeaton Station). The trackbed can then be followed to Macmerry Station (6.6 miles from Smeaton Station). The Macmerry branch ran parallel to an old horse tramway which carried coal from the Penston and other mines as well as pig iron from the iron furnaces at Gladsmuir to the east of Macmerry. The iron furnaces near the village gave it the nickname of 'The Blast'. A new National Coal Board Colliery at Winton, opened in 1950, lay almost immediately to the left after leaving Ormiston Junction and its closure in 1961 marked the effective end of the Macmerry branch which had been kept open as far as the mine. The line was used for the occasional special for railway enthusiasts.

The route is easily followed for the first mile beyond Ormiston Station along a minor road crossing the Puddle Burn and heading through woods. Where the trackbed cuts sharply north-east towards the site of Winton Station the Pentcaitland Sidings were located just over half-a-mile from Ormiston Junction. This was the site of the original Pencaitland Colliery and must have caused confusion with the

Macmerry looking to deadend

nearby Pencaitland Station on the Gifford line. The sidings were to the right of the trackbed near to Winton West Mains cottages. A farmer has reclaimed the section where the railway curved across his field and the walker is forced to reach the B6355 Pencaitland to Tranent road before following it north to Winton Station. The abutments of the former railway bridge over the line remain and in the field to the east can be traced the station site (432704). The simple station building was a wooden structure on a brick base with a hipped roof and beside it was a level crossing. The station was closed in 1925 and had three sidings and a loading bank. The last section to Macmerry had further mineral lines which branched east towards the Dander Pit, the Engine and Merryfield Pits and the Gladsmuir Iron Works which closed in 1882. Also branching to the east just before Macmerry and terminating north of the village were the Penston Pits. One mineral line ran just to the right of the Macmerry terminus and crossed the A1 Edinburgh to London road before reaching Penston No2 pit which closed in 1914.

From Ormiston, the railway climbed about thirty feet to reach Macmerry exposed on high ground overlooking the Firth. Tranent is only a short distance to the west and Haddington a few miles to the east. The terminus at Macmerry (433722) beside the A1 consisted of a single platform to the left and a modest waiting room with a simple station building. The passenger services stopped in 1925 since the train service of two trains per weekday with an extra running on Saturday attracted an average of only one passenger per trip. The buses to Tranent and Haddington were quicker and more direct. In the last days of the branch, the freight train from Macmerry carried only grain, potatoes and sugar beet and returned with fertiliser. The coal mining and iron working at the Blast had long ceased and the railway could no longer be justified.

Ormiston Junction from Puddle Bridge - Macmerry branch to left, Gifford branch to right - 1955

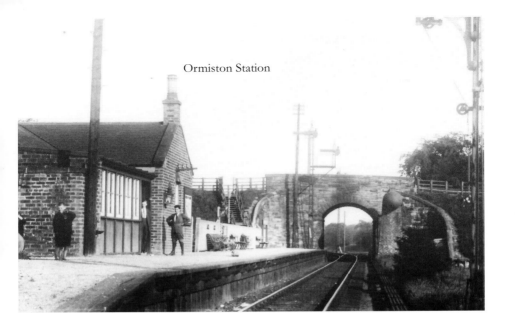

Ormiston Station

Ormiston Station to Saltoun Station

The railway walkway continues from Ormiston Junction east of Puddle Bridge where the railway to Gifford began. There were stations on this section at Pencaitland (5.9 miles from Smeaton Station) and Saltoun (7.6 miles from Smeaton Station).

The Macmerry and Gifford branches quickly diverge with the Gifford branch turning south and passing to the east of Ormiston and a large grain store. Only a concrete plaque to the side of the trackbed indicates where Meadow Pit, operated by the Ormiston Coal Company, was located. Sunk in 1890 and opened in 1903, it was abandoned by 1914. A few years before its closure, 110 men were employed. The sidings used by the colliery to the right of the trackbed continued in use for storing wagons for sixteen years after the pit closed. The grain store takes its name from the pit. The trackbed crosses a minor road at what was once the East Mains level crossing but which now leads to a sewage plant. Embedded in the tarmac of the road are two rails which are probably a remnant of the level crossing. The line rises towards the first railway bridge on the line which crosses the Tyne. The three-arched sandstone-faced bridge has brick-lined skewed arches on sandstone piers. As the line rises, the trackbed enters a deep cutting and then passes under the A6093 Dalkeith to Haddington road at Red Row. At this site, the Marchioness of Tweeddale cut the first sod of the Gifford branch on 8th April 1899. Road realignment has removed the bridge but the former trackbed is clearly seen on the far side of the road.

The trackbed then runs alongside the Black Wood which contains the few remains of Woodhall Colliery and is where the sidings were located. This pit which was also known as the Tyneholm Colliery or the Pencaitland Colliery was sunk in 1852 but was not fully exploited until 1903. The pit survived until 1944 and employed 198 men towards the end of its life. An eighty-foot long platform was provided for the workers just south of the Red Row Bridge. The Woodhall Colliery Company Platform bore no name board and its construction was subsidised by the company to the sum of fifty pounds. A third class workmen's only service was provided at 6.10am starting at Macmerry and dropping workmen off at Winton, Ormiston and Woodhall before running on to Gifford where the train was used to provide the first train of the day from Gifford to Edinburgh. The return trip was at 3.30pm. The experiment was not a success and the service was stopped just over four and a half months after it opened.

Beyond Red Row road bridge, the level crossings were un-gated since the regulations for Light Railways were not so restrictive. The first un-gated level crossing was next to Woodhall platform and the lack of gates contributed to a bad accident. A fish merchant, Thomas Nicholson from Longniddry, was killed in July 1924 when he misjudged the speed of the approaching Gifford-bound train and the truck he was driving was smashed in the collision.

The next section towards Pencaitland Station and on towards the summit at Lempock Wells Siding, with a gradient of one in fifty, is surprisingly steep and must have contributed to the leisurely pace of the trains. The first train from Gifford took almost one and a half hours to cover ten miles - about seven miles an hour!

The site of Broomrig or Branders Siding lies just before the grain silos of Bairds' malting which dominate the trackbed and emit eerie grinding sounds. The siding was used by contractors during the construction of the line and was sometimes known simply as the 'Workshop'. In the lee of the silos all that remains of Pencaitland Station is a gradient marker. The station master's house has recently been demolished. The small ticket office and platform have gone as have the two sidings and loading bank which stood where a car park and silos are now situated. Summer fruits such as strawberries were loaded on to trains here. The former station site is accessed along a track beside the entrance to the maltings.

The village of Pencaitland has expanded towards the trackbed from the east. Beyond the village, the railway crosses over the Pencaitland to Fountainhall road by a bridge which has been raised a few feet. Huntlaw Colliery, operated by Fletchers of Saltoun, was located to the right on this section but there is no evidence that it used the railway.

Pencaitland Stationmaster's house (now demolished) and gradient marker

The climb towards Lempock Wells Sidings eases only slightly to 1 in 58 as the siding is approached. The siding, also known as Fletcher's Siding and used by the Saltoun Estate, is barely discernible. The trackbed slightly widens at this point where it peaks and then starts to lose height. Lempock Wells Farm is immediately to the east and beyond the siding, a road bridge crosses over the line. The views towards the Lammermuirs over open fields, often of barley (in season), are good but are more restricted now by the growth of trees along the route. As the railway rapidly loses height, it passes under Milton access bridge with twin brick piers now replacing the original wooden supports. The Glenkinchie Distillery with its distinctive aroma (depending on the direction of the wind) lies in a narrow valley to the west and to the right its high chimney can be spotted. It produces one of Diageo's classic malts. There was no direct link from the railway to the distillery, whisky being transferred by road to Saltoun Station.

The trackbed then crosses over the Kinchie burn on a high embankment before passing over a minor road by a level crossing to reach the site of Saltoun Station (454666) The station was located about a mile from West Saltoun and even further from East Saltoun The station house remains but the sidings, goods yard and passing loop which were located to the south of the station have been removed along with the ticket office and platforms. Goods traffic consisted of the usual agricultural produce but more importantly for the viability of the line, the local distillery required about ten tons of coal a day and that coal along with many of the raw ingredients, such as barley, was brought in by train. The finished product in the form of barrels of whisky was carried to Edinburgh by the railway.

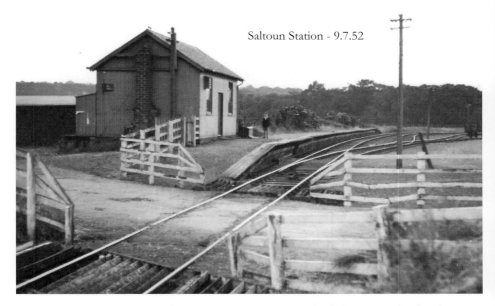

Saltoun Station - 9.7.52

The car park at the site of the station marks the end of the Pencaitland railway walk. A pleasant detour, west along the road taking first right, leads to Glenkinchie Distillery. The 'Glen' was added later to make the distillery seem more Scottish. The Glenkinchie, usually bottled at ten years and marketed as the Edinburgh Malt, is one of the few remaining examples of the lighter Lowland style. Guided tours finishing with a dram are available throughout the day.

Saltoun to Gifford

There were stations on this section at Humbie (9.7 miles from Smeaton Junction) and Gifford (13.5 miles from Smeaton Junction). The Humbie Viaduct has been demolished and the route is difficult to follow other than in short sections. South of Saltoun Station, the railway lost more height for about a quarter of a mile before beginning an almost continuous climb, often at a gradient of 1 in 50 for over two miles to reach the site of the Humbie Viaduct (459661) over Humbie Water. Only slight traces of the four arch viaduct in a deep, narrow and heavily wooded gorge remain. It was 150 feet in length and 48 feet high. The site of the viaduct can be found at the north-eastern edge of the Saltoun Forest and can be accessed by the road heading south from Saltoun Station turning left at the cottages at Old Duncrahill and following a minor road.

South of the former viaduct, the trackbed snakes along the edge of woods before turning sharply east. Highlea Siding which served Lord Polwarth's estate at

Humbie House was located where the trackbed changes direction. This section can only be accessed from the site of the former Humbie Station. The site (481651) is two miles east of Humbie village along the B6368. Next to the road are the Humbie Station cottages. The disused platform and sidings can be located in the woods to the east of the trackbed. Although the goods traffic at Humbie was mainly agricultural, pit props were also carried from the station.

One eccentric commuter travelled from Humbie Station each morning. He allowed his chauffeur to drop him off at the station in his Rolls-Royce and then travelled by train to Edinburgh where the same chauffeur picked him up and took him to his office. This was made possible by an unusual feature of this light railway whereby the trains on the line didn't stop at the end of the light railway but were allowed to continue on to the main line to Edinburgh. Immediately to the east of the station, the railway crossed the Birns Water by a bridge close to Gilchriston Farm. This single-arched bridge was washed away in the floods of 1948 isolating the line near Gifford forever.

The next section of the trackbed is lost until near How Knowe two miles east and then south of the B6368 where the former railway can be rediscovered running beside the How Burn and the narrow Howburn Wood. From here, the trackbed heads towards Gifford crossing the B6355 Saltoun to Gifford road by a level crossing before running beside the Speedy Burn until it reaches Speedy Wood and eventually the terminus about a third of a mile from Gifford. This last section is easily traced but the station at Gifford (529683) is in private grounds. No horse-drawn carriage now awaits a train to take the traveller into the village but the walk to the village is pleasant and the hospitality whilst waiting for the bus is warm.

Gifford Station looking towards Edinburgh

For around twenty years, the Gifford railway remained independent and a rival to road transport. It even made a contribution to the war effort when local children collected sacks of rose hips which were sent by train to Newcastle to be turned into healthy rosehip syrup. The passenger service stopped as early as 1933 but the goods service was withdrawn in stages. Although the section of railway between Gifford and Humbie was closed when the bridge near Gilchriston farm was washed away in the severe floods of 1948, Gifford Station continued to be served by road from Haddington Station until it was finally closed on January 1st 1959. The railway was cut back to Saltoun Station in 1960 with Pencaitland Station closing in 1964 and finally the whole line from Smeaton in 1965.

The wrong choice of route through a thinly populated area, difficult gradients, the closing of the coal mines and the rise of the motor car, all contributed to the demise of the light railway to Gifford. The railway walk preserves an important part of the trackbed and is probably busier now than it has ever been.

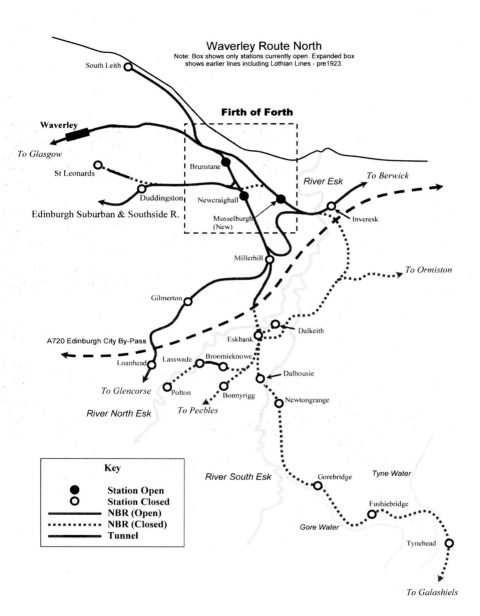

Waverley Route North

Note: Box shows only stations currently open. Expanded box shows earlier lines including Lothian Lines - pre1923.

South Leith

Firth of Forth

Waverley

To Glasgow

St Leonards

Brunstane

River Esk

To Berwick

Duddingston

Newcraighall

Inveresk

Edinburgh Suburban & Southside R.

Musselburgh (New)

To Ormiston

Millerhill

Gilmerton

A720 Edinburgh City By-Pass

Dalkeith

Eskbank

Loanhead

Lasswade

Broomieknowe

Dalhousie

To Glencorse

Polton

Bonnyrigg

Newtongrange

To Peebles

River North Esk

River South Esk

Gorebridge

Tyne Water

Fushiebridge

Gore Water

Tynehead

To Galashiels

Key	
●	**Station Open**
○	**Station Closed**
——	**NBR (Open)**
∙∙∙∙∙∙	**NBR (Closed)**
——	**Tunnel**

Chapter 2

The Waverley Route from Edinburgh to Falahill Summit : including the St Leonards, Musselburgh, Dalkeith and Lothian Lines

The re-opening of the Waverley route to Tweedbank near Galashiels could partially restore a greatly missed rail link to the Scottish Borders, the largest area in Europe without a station. A re-opened line would allow passengers to commute between the Borders and Edinburgh, relieving pressure on the road system, and could help to regenerate the economies of both Midlothian and the Borders. It is unlikely, however, that any of the branches from the route will re-open but their history and that of the Waverley Route in Edinburgh and the Lothians is worth exploring.

The original reason behind the network of railways that eventually evolved from the Edinburgh and Dalkeith Railway (EDR) network to become the Waverley Route, under the guidance of the North British Railway Company (NBR), was the insatiable demand for coal from the Lothian coalfields by the townsfolk and business interests in the capital. 'Auld Reekie' needed a reliable and plentiful supply of coal. The EDR, a system of horse drawn waggonways, provided the means. Coal and a vision of a third Anglo-Scottish route serving the Border towns and rivalling the East Coast and West Coast Main Lines led to the construction of the Waverley Route.

Edinburgh and Dalkeith Railway

The Edinburgh and Dalkeith opened between Edinburgh St Leonards and Eskbank in July 1831, which made it the earliest of the other pioneering routes such as the Glasgow and Garnkirk (opened in September 1831) and the Dundee and Newtyle (opened in December 1831). Support from landowners, eager to deliver coal from their estates to Edinburgh, led to the EDR developing quickly from a base at St Leonards beside Salisbury Crags. Given that the coal was being delivered to the terminus in Edinburgh, it might have been more appropriate to call the railway the Dalkeith and Edinburgh. There were many obstacles and technical challenges as it headed eastwards towards Niddrie. One of the first railway tunnels in Scotland had to be hewn out of rock only yards from the Edinburgh terminus and the bridge over the Braid Burn, built in 1831, is one of the earliest surviving cast iron structures of its type. For the coal to reach the terminus, stationary steam engines had to be used to haul coal up a one in thirty inclined plane worked by ropes. For the rest of the route, horse drawn wagons were used. Indeed, the railway became known as the Innocent Railway partly because of its refusal to use steam locomotives instead of horses, a policy which did not change until the company was taken over by the NBR in 1845.

The line from St Leonards reached Niddrie Junction Station from where routes diverged in several directions. The first route to be opened reached south to Eskbank in 1831 and the same year, a mile and a half long branch was constructed to the harbour at Fisherrow, near Musselburgh. The Fisherrow branch provided a freight service and a passenger service which proved popular with local fishwives.

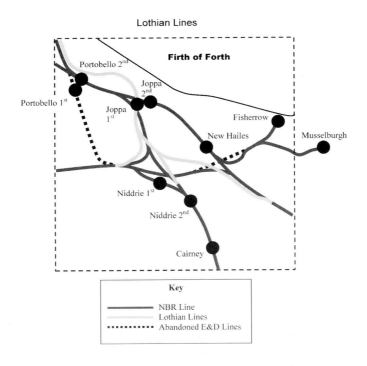

40

The Edinburgh and Dalkeith's attitude towards passengers could also be called innocent. When the manager, David Rankine, was asked by Lord Seymour's Railway Select Committee of 1839: "How do you take your tickets on the Dalkeith Railway?", his reply was: "We do not use them. There are so many different places for lifting passengers; it is a very populous country; there are a great many villages and we have always found that many persons would not tell or did not make up their minds where they were going which causes great confusion in using tickets." Changed days! However the byelaws did forbid drivers from grazing their horses whilst pulling trains! Incidentally, the EDR did not use its own rolling stock or motive power. It was 'franchised' out.

South of Niddrie, there were further stations at Cairney (from where the Edmonstone Waggonway ran westwards to Little France) and Sheriffhall. It then crossed the River North Esk by a sixty foot span bridge to reach   where there was a short branch to Dalkeith, the last part of the EDR network to open. A private waggonway linked up with the Dalkeith terminus and was used to carry coals from mines to the east of Dalkeith requiring the construction of the Victoria Viaduct across the River South Esk at Thorneybank. Continuing south from Dalkeith, the railway ended at South Esk Station near Dalhousie, blocked temporarily by the River South Esk. The gorge was a formidable barrier but funding from the Marquis of Lothian and the attraction of the coalfields around Arniston, to the south of the river, led to the construction in 1832 of a 340 foot timber structure resting on iron arches and sandstone piers.

The EDR also expanded northward to Portobello and Leith harbour in 1838. Once again this route originated near Niddrie, the central hub for the Edinburgh and Dalkeith's operations.

Niddrie North Junction - 23.10.71
Waverley route to left; suburban line to right; Lothian lines on high level

North British Railway and the Waverley Route

The EDR was a valuable coal line for the capital and was also carrying passengers in increasing numbers. It was an attractive target for the expanding NBR who took it over in 1845, paying less for it and its branches than they cost to construct. The NBR standardised the gauge (the gap between the rails) at four feet eight and three quarter inches and introduced trains hauled by steam locomotives where possible - the horse drawn waggonways were being modernised. The NBR also used the North Bridge General Station, later Waverley Station, and by 1847 St Leonards had been relegated to a goods depot without a passenger service. There were, however, several unsuccessful attempts to re-introduce a passenger timetable.

The first southerly extension introduced by the NBR was a Hawick service which opened in 1849 with the line leaving the Edinburgh to Berwick line at Portobello East Junction and joining the old EDR line at what became Niddrie South Junction. Around Niddrie, many changes were made and the EDR line to Portobello and Leith harbour was abandoned. A new station was built at Niddrie further to the south, better positioned for the new section of track from Portobello East Junction. There were further changes to the location and number of stations on the new route. South of Cairney Station, the line was re-aligned to create a more direct route. New stations were opened at Millerhill in 1849 on the newly built section of track and also further south at Gallowshall in 1847, re-named Eskbank in 1850. Cairney and Sheriffhall Stations were closed in 1846 and then briefly re-opened. South Esk Station was renamed Dalhousie in 1847.

The original timber viaduct across the River South Esk, south of Eskbank, funded by the Marquis of Lothian, was replaced by the stronger and wider twenty-two arch Newbattle Viaduct built of brick and stone. South of the viaduct, Newtongrange Station opened in 1908 when Dalhousie Station closed and was overlooked by and linked to, the Lady Victoria Colliery which began operations in 1895. The Waverley Route then turned south east and passed through Gorebridge and Fushiebridge before reaching the most demanding gradients on the section at Borthwick Bank. This was a difficult four mile climb at one in seventy, passing the remote station at Tynehead before reaching the summit at Falahill almost nine hundred feet above sea-level.

From Portobello East Junction to Falahill Summit, the route climbed continuously for almost the entire length of the Waverley Route in the Lothians creating difficult conditions for both engines and crews. The bad news for the crews was that there was worse to come at Whitrope, further south, where the trains had to surmount an even higher summit.

The Waverley Route then headed down the valley of the Gala Water passing through Heriot Station just over a mile from Falahill Summit and stations at Stow and Bowland before reaching Galashiels. Inevitably, the presence of the Waverley route created a demand for branch lines to nearby towns anxious not to be left out. The status of existing branches was also altered. As already mentioned, when the line from Portobello East to Niddrie South Junction was opened, the St Leonards section of the EDR was relegated to branch status.

The Fisherrow branch was extended to Musselburgh and the NBR linked it to the Edinburgh to Berwick line, the first route constructed by the NBR. They built another branch from Monktonhall Junction on the Edinburgh to Berwick line south to Smeaton which is to the north east of Dalkeith and on to Thorneybank in 1866. This line was extended in the following year to reach the Waverley Route at Hardengreen. The route used part of the old waggonway system around Victoria Viaduct which served Dalkeith.

A route was built to Peebles via Leadburn. This branched south west from Hardengreen Junction just south of Eskbank Station. Eventually it was extended through the Tweed Valley before rejoining the Waverley line just east of Galashiels, forming a loop. Branching from the Peebles loop was the short spur to Polton and the branch to Penicuik. The Glencorse Railway left the Waverley Route south of Millerhill. These routes are covered in the chapter on the 'Railways of the North Esk Valley'.

Musselburgh

A branch of the EDR system from the first Niddrie Station headed north-east to Fisherrow Harbour, the port for Musselburgh. The one and a half mile branch was opened in October 1831 and ended on the quayside at Fisherrow Harbour. Three years later, a passenger service was started which proved popular despite the passenger carriages being uncovered.

When the NBR took control of the Edinburgh and Dalkeith network in 1845, the line to Fisherrow was re-aligned with the first three quarters of a mile abandoned and a new junction provided on the Edinburgh to Berwick route. Newhailes Junction (324721) was constructed to meet up with the old line to Fisherrow. In July 1847, the line was extended south-east across the River Esk to a new terminus in Musselburgh (340725) The Fisherrow branch reverted to freight traffic only and survived until 1961.

Records show three stations with the name of Musselburgh. The first opened in June 1846 on the Edinburgh to Berwick line and lay to the south-east of the town. It was re-named Inveresk when the new NBR terminal opened. Inveresk Station was re-named Inveresk Junction in October 1876 and reverted to Inveresk in June 1890 before finally closing in May 1964.

43

The new NBR station in Musselburgh was an elaborate affair with a tall stone frontage, opening on to a large forecourt, with features such as mock battlements over the entrance foyer. The facilities included a single platform partly covered by a wooden roof. There was an engine shed (closed in 1930) and a siding serving local wireworks, an important industry in the town. Another of Musselburgh's staple industries, paper production, also used the railways. Slightly to the south of the station was the last paper mill before the mouth of the River Esk and its location on the east bank was probably the reason why the railway crossed the river. From Penicuik to Musselburgh, the River Esk provided water to power the paper mills and helped to create an important industry.

Passengers travelling between North Bridge Station, Edinburgh and Musselburgh in June 1846 were offered a range of first class, second class and third class carriages, all painted in claret. The first class carriages were divided into six person compartments based on stage coach designs and, mercifully, even the third class carriages offered protection from the weather. Fifteen trains were timetabled, ten of them local, in addition to the five return trips to Berwick which also stopped at Musselburgh. The railway was a success, carrying almost a million passengers a year in the 1920s. In 1850, there were eight trains a day operating between Musselburgh and Edinburgh and fifty years later there was an average of two trains per hour. This continued until the passenger service was withdrawn in 1964. All traffic ceased in 1971.

Nothing remains of the route. The station buildings have been demolished and the A6095 road has been re-aligned. The last half mile towards the terminus is now Olive Bank Road, and the bridge over the River Esk is part of a busy road network. The section from Newhailes Junction, although still shown on maps curving south of an industrial estate, is difficult to trace and a walk down Olive Bank Road provides a very tenuous connection to the railway. In October 1988, a new Musselburgh Station located on the ECML was opened and is proving very popular with commuters.

Dalkeith

Dalkeith had been in existence for almost seven hundred years and was already a thriving market town before its first brush with the railway era when the EDR line reached the town on a spur from its main route. This spur, opened in 1839, was wholly owned by the Duke of Buccleuch and although it was intended as a gift for the use of the town, it also provided a route for coal to leave his estates. When the NBR took over the EDR network, Dalkeith became a short half-mile branch from

Glenesk Junction. From the station in Dalkeith, the Duke constructed a horse-drawn tramway known as the Buccleuch Tramway. It passed through the streets of Dalkeith, which meant demolishing several properties en route, towards the very ornate Victoria Viaduct over the River South Esk to reach Thorneybank and then to the Duke's coalfields to the east of the town at Smeaton and Cowden. A siding serviced the Mushet ironworks which were closer to the station.

The coalfields east of Dalkeith attracted further development from the NBR who built a branch from the ECML at Monktonhall Junction, near Inveresk, south to Smeaton. From here, a branch was constructed east to Macmerry near Tranent and later Gifford, a remote village, in the foothills of the Lammermuirs. These routes are described in the chapter on the railways of East Lothian. With enthusiastic support from the people of Dalkeith, track was laid from Smeaton south-west through Dalkeith to reach the Waverley Route at Hardengreen Junction near Eskbank. The branch from Smeaton to Eskbank was opened throughout in 1870 but was always under-used and closed in 1934.

Lothian Lines

By 1913, the volume of coal traffic towards the port at Leith was causing a bottleneck at Portobello. The charges imposed by the NBR also provoked resentment for the inadequate service provided and the response of local coal mine owners was to promote their own series of lines using their own engines and wagons including the construction of a causeway into the Firth of Forth at Seafield near the South Leith terminus. The NBR defeated their attempts and promised to upgrade the service. During 1915, a new line was completed from Seafield climbing towards Portobello and sweeping round the existing goods yard before crossing the ECML and the Waverley Route. The new line then split with a spur west to Niddrie West Junction and the other branch splitting again to reach Niddrie South Junction and then Niddrie East Junction. It was a good solution, even though the earthworks were considerable, since it reduced congestion at the docks, bypassed the bottleneck at Portobello and linked to existing lines. The Lothian lines were to prove a great success before declining levels of traffic led to their closure in 1967.

Decline and Closure

After a brief attempt to reintroduce passenger services in 1860 which lasted only four months, the St Leonards branch then closed for passengers permanently although a goods service continued until 1968 over a hundred years longer. Hardengreen to Smeaton closed for freight in 1934. Passenger traffic on the short Glenesk Junction to Dalkeith branch ceased in 1942 but a goods service was maintained until 1964. The Waverley Route went into decline by being gradually shorn of its feeder branches and losing most of the goods traffic from the mill towns of Galashiels and Hawick along with the important livestock trade. Its use from the 1960s as an express freight route was undermined by the general decline of freight traffic on the railway network. The British Railways Modernisation Plan led to the opening of Millerhill Yard, in June 1962, to cope with the still considerable local coal traffic and to link with a similar goods yard at Carlisle Kingmoor at the southern end of the Waverley Route. Millerhill replaced the freight yards at Portobello and Niddrie. Millerhill Station had already closed in 1955.

After a long and emotional rearguard action by supporters of the Waverley Route, the line was closed as a through route on 5th January 1969 and by early 1972 the track south of Newtongrange had been lifted. Due to the coal traffic from the Lady Victoria Colliery, the section from Edinburgh to Newtongrange was kept open until December 1971.

The proposals for the re-opened line from Edinburgh to Galashiels and Tweedbank envisage stations, in the Lothian section, at Brunstane (9 miles from Waverley Station), Newcraighall (13), Shawfair (16), Eskbank (20), Newtongrange (24) and Gorebridge (30). Both Brunstane and Newcraighall have already been opened.

Exploring the Railway Heritage

All the routes in this chapter are covered by the following maps; Landranger 66; Explorer 345 and 350.

St Leonards - the Innocent Railway

The St Leonards branch forms part of a walkway and cycle path. Only the end sections have been changed. At the east end, the connection to the Southside Suburban Circle at Duddingston Junction (290721) has been removed along with Duddingston and Craigmillar Station which was to the south of the junction. At the other end, St Leonards terminus has been built on. Not far away, at just over 1.7 miles, the walkway lies in the shadow of Arthur's Seat, part of Holyrood Park

The start is at the site of Cairntows level crossing (287721) where the railway crosses the Duddingston Road. There is still a white level crossing gate (although not the original) and the walkway almost immediately enters between two stone walls. The higher stone wall to the left protects walkers from stray golf balls from Duddingston Golf Course. A sign beside the wall proclaims the 'Innocent Railway'. Another sign tells of one of the earliest cast iron bridges built in 1831 by James Jardine who engineered the EDR. Part of the bridge remains in the centre of the walkway, with the curved beams on top protruding above the level of the walkway. The stone walls to either side restrict views but Craigmillar Castle can be seen to the left with the Royal Observatory on Blackford Hill further west. Due to trees, little can be seen of Duddingston Village on the eastern slopes of Holyrood Park and even less of Duddingston Loch with its Bawsinch Wildlife Reserve. Straight ahead looms Arthur's Seat and the spur of rock that necessitated the construction of the 556 yard St Leonards tunnel. The tunnel, twenty feet wide and fifteen feet high, now lit by electric and not gas lamps, is a testimony to the skills of James Jardine. It is soot-encrusted from the steam locomotives which eventually used the tunnel when rope working on the incline ceased. The tunnel climbs steeply at 1 in 30 which was very difficult for horses and the wagons were initially hauled up the incline by rope using two stationary winding engines. Loads of thirty tons could be hauled up the incline. Beyond the tunnel was St Leonards Terminus (265727) which covered eight acres and consisted largely of sidings to collect coal. Warehouses dominated the terminus to the east and passenger facilities were scant. The terminus site is now occupied by flats and the walk ends at the entrance to Holyrood Park. A climb up Arthur's Seat provides a good overview of this section of Edinburgh's pioneering railway.

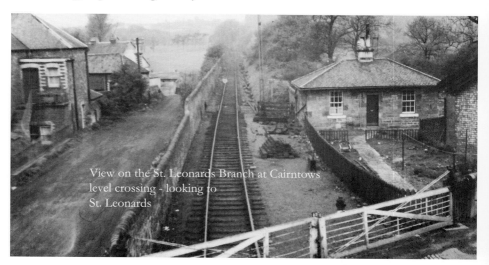

View on the St. Leonards Branch at Cairntows level crossing - looking to St. Leonards

The Waverley Route and branches south of the Edinburgh City Bypass

The builders of the Edinburgh City Bypass did not share the optimism of those seeking to re-open the line. Although they built a bridge over the Glencorse route, they did not build one over the disused trackbed of the former Waverley Route and the rails stop north of the bypass. Exploration of the route should be started south of the bypass. If the trackbed is explored, starting from the short spur of the Dalkeith Branch, it is walkable to the Edinburgh City Bypass from Glenesk Viaduct. Turning south from Glenesk Junction, Eskbank Station (1 mile) is soon passed and the railway can be walked to the site of Hardengreen Junction (1.5 miles) which is behind the Tesco Store. A footbridge allows access to the Peebles loop and the trackbed of this railway can then be walked to Penicuik (9.2 miles) (see the chapter on the 'Railways of the North Esk Valley'). Further south, a new section of the A7 cuts through the trackbed before the fenced-off Newbattle Viaduct is reached.

The next section that can be walked begins beside the Lady Victoria coal mine, now a museum, and can be followed to Gorebridge but there are gaps and the A7 has to be crossed. From Gorebridge, the route can be followed to Falahill but some sections can be difficult due to conditions underfoot and transport has to be arranged to return to your starting point. There is a regular bus service from Falahill and Heriot. Only short sections of the railway branch from Hardengreen Junction to Monktonhall Junction now remain and the Victoria Viaduct has been demolished. North of Thorneybank Industrial Estate, the Penicuik to Musselburgh Foot and Cycleway uses the former trackbed.

Dalkeith Station to Glenesk Viaduct

The short half-mile route is almost intact and is a pleasant walkway from near the site of the former Dalkeith Station on Eskbank Road which is now a bus station. The station was closed in January 1942 and nothing remains of it. Beside the bus garage, car hire premises are also built on the trackbed. A short distance west, the route is discovered, opposite St David's RC Church, at the site of a former overbridge over the line (327669) which eventually leads to a cemetery. Along the Cemetery Road is a tall distinctive former water tower. The iron tank at the top of the octagonal brick tower has been removed to create a most unusual house with panoramic views.

Dalkeith Station looking to deadend

The railway walk to Glenesk Viaduct is signposted. Easy access at the overbridge leads to the old railway trackbed which is now a tree-lined path. From the overbridge, the route swung north-west towards Glenesk Viaduct (324671). To the right is the deep gorge created by the River North Esk with views over Ironmills Park. The site of Glenesk Junction where the short Dalkeith branch reached the Waverley Route has been landscaped and the signal box removed. The former Waverley Route has also been made into a pathway and the Dalkeith branch is a good starting point to explore this section of it.

Glenesk Viaduct, built in 1847, has a single large semicircular masonry arch. Due to mining subsidence, it has been strengthened with steel. The bridge is listed Grade B. The surface of the bridge and path has been tarmacadamed and the addition of metal railings has allowed the transformation of the bridge from railway to walkway. To the west, a new road carries the A7 and between it and the railway is Elginhaugh road bridge. To the east, beyond Ironmills Park, are the Scottish Qualification Board premises in the Ironmills Industrial Park, a venue which strikes fear into many a Scottish pupil and teacher. The area is named after an iron foundry which supplied the Duke of Buccleuch and many local mines and grain mills with ironmongery.

Glenesk Junction signalbox

North of the viaduct, the Waverley Route entered a deep and wide tree-lined cutting before passing under the A68 where the cycle path veers north-west towards Edinburgh. The line then curved north-east running alongside the western boundary of Dalkeith Country Park, the location of Dalkeith House which was the main residence of the Duke of Buccleuch until 1916. Many royal visitors, including Queen Victoria, enjoyed the Duke's hospitality here.

The trackbed stops next to the Edinburgh bypass and you should retrace your steps.

Waverley Route - Glenesk Junction to Newbattle Viaduct

Glenesk Junction was close to where the railway walk from Dalkeith and the cycle path from the south meet. Leaving the Dalkeith walkway and turning south, the tarmac path leads past the site of sidings to the right and heads towards Eskbank Station which is beyond an overbridge. The station was known as Eskbank and Dalkeith from 1954. Set in a cutting, the station is clearly recognisable with its long platforms and still retains many of the original station buildings and the remains of a shelter to the right, next to another overbridge. Between the two road bridges is a metal footbridge. The station site (324666) is remarkably unchanged and it doesn't take a lot of imagination to picture trains stopping here again but that is not in the re-opening plans. The offices and station house were at road level and the two storey ashlar buildings remain with a shop attached. The site can be accessed from Lasswade Road. If the railway re-opens, the new Eskbank Station will be located further south.

Eskbank and Dalkeith Station looking south

Eskbank Station platforms today

Beyond the next overbridge which carries the Bonnyrigg road bridge, housing encroaches to the right of the trackbed and a landscaped embankment to the left. This was the site of Hardengreen Junction (323662). The start of the line to Smeaton departed north east but due to landscaping is not today easily identified. The start of the line is a landscaped embankment. To the left, there was an engine shed providing banking engines for the hard climb to the south. This shed has been demolished and the site is now part of a business centre. The junction for the Peebles loop left to the south west. The site was overlooked by a very tall three-storey brick signal box with the top storey protruding towards the line to offer good views over a busy junction. Only the name of the business centre, with the platforms of Eskbank and Dalkeith Station beyond, link the scene to the past. For many years after the closure of the Smeaton branch, a short siding was retained and was known as "the Hole" where banking engines, used for the long haul to Falahill Summit, could be stored.

The trackbed now passes behind the Tesco Store with ever improving views over the Esk valley to the west and north to the Moorfoot Hills. This is the site of the proposed Eskbank Station. The cycleway leaves the former trackbed on the original approaches to Newbattle Viaduct and winds back to a new footbridge over the A7. It then picks up the trackbed of the Peebles loop as it runs towards the Esk Valley Junction and Bonnyrigg.

Newbattle Viaduct to Gorebridge

The A7 runs beside the Newbattle Viaduct before winding under the most southerly arch and heading up towards Newtongrange. The viaduct, also known as Lothianbridge, is fenced off but the twenty two brick and sandstone arches dominate the gorge. A caravan park sits under the arches. Dalhousie Station was immediately to the north of the viaduct. The platforms have been removed from this station, closed in 1908, but the station building remains. The original viaduct was slightly to the east and some remains can still be seen next to the minor road which leads to Dalhousie Mains. A massive embankment to the south of the viaduct now leads into a scrapyard. The trackbed then enters a cutting and winds between rows of miners' cottages before once more passing under the A7. On the far side of the bridge was the site of Newtongrange Station (332641). If the route is re-opened, the station will be rebuilt in the vee between the road and the trackbed. The booking office was at road level in the original station with a footbridge connecting the two platforms. On each side, canopies with deep valances projected from the waiting rooms to provide shelter for waiting passengers.

The station site is still dominated by the Lady Victoria Colliery, now preserved as the home of the Scottish Mining Museum and well worth a visit to understand the difficult working conditions that miners experienced. The colliery overlooks Midlothian with views towards the Pentland Hills and Edinburgh. The pit opened in 1895 and was named after the wife of the then Marquis of Lothian. Part of the Newbattle collieries, it continued a tradition of coal-mining in the area probably begun in the sixteenth century. To the east of the Lady Victoria was Lingerwood Colliery which remain connected by a concrete walkway. The southern part of the site contained the workshops for the collieries. Newtongrange still consists of many traditional miners' rows although substantially upgraded. The houses in the miners' rows were once tied to employment in the mines but were provided with piped water and sanitation which was an improvement in standards. The collieries had their own railway network connecting Lady Victoria, Lingerwood and Easthouses to the north east. Near Newtongrange Station, but on the opposite side of the Waverley Route from the Lady Victoria Colliery, was the Newbattle Stocking Site, now a housing estate.

The line runs beside the colliery site towards Brewer's Bush overbridge. The area is in need of redevelopment with, at present, many scars from its industrial past remaining. Beyond the overbridge are several more overbridges before the route enters the wooded gorge of the Gore Water where the trackbed is lost as it begins to turn south east. Further on, the rail bridge over the A7 has also gone but the trackbed can be picked up just to the north of the new road bridge, called Shank Bridge, over the Gore Water at the top of a steep embankment. Here, there were more collieries at Arniston, the original terminus of the old EDR. When the EDR worked the coals on the eastern edge of the Midlothian coalfield, the pits were shallow but in 1860 the Arniston Emily pit was sunk to enable access to more valuable coal seams and, at that time, it was the deepest in the east of Scotland. Later, the Arniston Coal Company was set up and further pits were developed such as the Gore pit which was sunk immediately beside the Waverley Route. Little evidence of the pits remains. The trackbed then passes the ruins of Newbyres Castle, to the north of the former line, before reaching Gorebridge.

Waverley Route - Gorebridge to Falahill Summit

The station site at Gorebridge (344613) is found beyond the road bridge which carries the steeply sloping Station Road over the former route. Most of Gorebridge is perched on the hillside above the station and a steep embankment, now overgrown with trees and bushes, runs down to the trackbed. Houses have been built on the station site where the sidings were located but there is a narrow path which allows access along the trackbed. Some of the platform can still be seen, embedded in the ground. The signal box which was on the left beyond Station Road has been removed but some of the original station buildings remain, now cleaned up. A short distance along, another road bridge crosses the line. The station site was cramped between the two road bridges but will still be used if the line is re-opened since there is really no other suitable site. Homeowners at the station site may be less than impressed. The station closed in 1969.

The trackbed continues in a deep cutting, sometimes requiring low stone

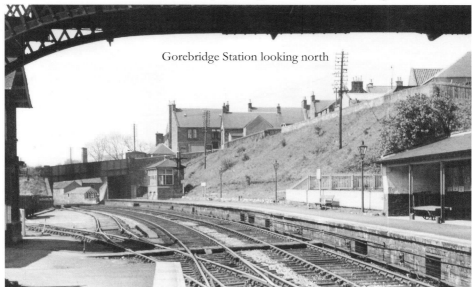

Gorebridge Station looking north

retaining walls. While a steeply-banked slope remains to the left, to the right it starts to slope away allowing views towards the Border hills and the village of Birkenside immediately to the west. Near Catcune Mills was Fushiebridge Station which was closed to passengers in 1943 and to goods in 1959. The station site (352323) is overgrown as is the trackbed. The station was beside a sloping road bridge near overbridge 29 across the railway.

Beyond Fushiebridge, a mineral line veered away to the south west, crossing the Gore water, to Castleton before turning south east to reach Esperton Lime Works. The Waverley Route was not quite out of the Midlothian coalfield since there was another spur to the left heading back behind Gorebridge to the Vogrie pit which, probably because it was the most southerly pit on the Waverley Route, supplied coal to the Border towns. The Waverley Route now entered a beautiful but isolated section as it started to snake its way towards the summit at Falahill. Known as Borthwick Bank, this four mile stretch on a gradient of one in seventy was a demanding climb for trains.

Near Catcune Farm, the access bridge to the farm has been filled in but there is no other obstacle as the trackbed changes from an embankment to a deep wide cutting. Cattle are the only companions as the line reaches the tiny hamlet of Borthwick. Borthwick Castle, a fifteenth century tower house over one hundred feet high, with historic links to Mary Queen of Scots and Oliver Cromwell, is now converted to a hotel. It was to Borthwick Castle that Mary Queen of Scots and the Earl of Bothwell fled after their disastrous runaway marriage. When it was besieged by Scottish nobles opposed to Mary in 1567, she managed to escape by disguising as a pageboy. The public records of Scotland were removed from Edinburgh and stored here during the Second World War.

One of the many attractions of the Waverley route were the contrasting landscapes through which it passed. From the suburban sprawl of Edinburgh climbing through the Midlothian coalfield and its tightly knit coal communities to reach open countryside, the surroundings were constantly changing. Borthwick Bank produced many memorable views of trains, frequently photographed and etched in travellers' memories. One very popular site for photographers was at the point where the trackbed is crossed by a road bridge near Borthwick. From the road at a tight U-bend, photographers would capture passing trains struggling against the incline in the deep wide cutting.

Beyond the road bridge, an embankment provides a good viewing platform in all directions and through the hills, Crichton Castle is seen to the north before the trackbed enters a deep cutting at Maggie Bowies Glen. The cutting is waterlogged in places and it is best to climb up the embankment to avoid the difficult conditions underfoot. Near an old farm access bridge, there is still a red British Railways Board sign indicating a weight limit of three tons for vehicles crossing the bridge.

Through the cutting, the trackbed turns south to reach an in-filled bridge. Take the high ground to reach the hamlet of Tynehead. To the south of the road bridge over the line, on the B6458, Tynehead Station (394592) is situated. Two platforms are still seen at the bottom of a deep cutting with access from each side. The main station buildings were at road level and are now a private residence. The station took its name from the nearby Tyne Water which starts near Tynehead. Originally named as Tyne Head, it opened in 1848, was re-named Tynehead in 1874 and closed with the Waverley Route in 1969. Beside the wing walls of the bridge was a simple hip-roofed waiting room, now demolished, accessed by a path from road level. One mile from the end of Borthwick Bank, the station was a lonely outpost of the railway empire.

The trackbed remains in a deep gully beyond Tynehead with trees closing in on both sides and growing on the trackbed itself, making conditions difficult again before the disused line emerges from the woods near Cowbraehill Farm and approaches the A7, last seen near Gorebridge. Crossing bleak moorland, considerable earthworks were required to construct an embankment before the summit was reached at Falahill. At the summit, there was a water tower to replenish the steam engines and a signal box to operate the extensive sidings which in the later years of the Waverley Route were largely unused. By 1965, the sidings were lifted and the signal box had been removed. The trackbed then becomes an access road which eventually emerges at the A7 behind some cottages. The road bridge over the trackbed has been removed and the road re-aligned. The trackbed can be continued to Heriot Station, a short distance down the valley of the Gala Water. From here it was downhill all the way to Galashiels.

Hardengreen Junction to Smeaton

Few traces remain of the railway from Smeaton to Hardengreen Junction. The junction site has been landscaped but a substantial length of cutting begins just north of Ancrum Road (327665) where Dalhousie Road meets it. A plate girder overbridge survives where Dalhousie Road crosses over the former railway track. The trackbed runs parallel to Ancrum Road and then Torsonce Road before ending just short of Abbey Road opposite a fire station. Abbey Road eventually becomes Lothian Road and just before it merges in turn with London Road, there is a short isolated section of trackbed between some buildings. Turning right on to London Road and then left to Newmills Road leads to a large car park behind a food store. The construction of the stone wall suggests that it might have been the perimeter wall of a railway site. Near here at Elmfield was the site of the ironworks owned by William Mushet which were served by a siding to the east of the railway. The siding was closed in 1894. The ironworks had also been served by the Buccleuch tramway. The Dalkeith gas works were also provided with sidings. Later, in 1910, closer to the Victoria Viaduct, the NBR opened the Telegraph Pole Siding or Gibraltar Sidings where they stored telegraph poles for use on the railways. Several streets still bear the name of Gibraltar in this area today.

A walk through the Gibraltar estate leads to Musselburgh Road. On the far side are the grounds of Dalkeith Park. Going east, the New Cow Bridge crosses the River South Esk and beside it is a new pedestrian bridge allowing safer passage for pupils walking to the joint Dalkeith Schools Community Campus. This whole area has changed dramatically. South of the road bridge was the site of Victoria Viaduct which was reconstructed when the Hardengreen to Smeaton branch was opened. The original viaduct, according to the New Statistical Account, consisted of six arches, each with a span of over a hundred feet built of the best Dantzick timber on stone piers of hewn ashlar. The elegant structure supported by timber arches was dramatic but, more practically, allowed the Duke access to the Cowden mines east of the river. The viaduct was named in honour of a visit by Queen Victoria to nearby Dalkeith Palace. The replacement was more practical. The timber arches were dismantled and the piers modified to support twin wrought iron girders. Some evidence of the piers remain in the ground leading down to the river. In 1940, the metal work was removed for scrap to support the war effort and in 1964 the piers were taken away.

Once over the river, the railway reached Thorneybank, now the site of an industrial estate, before heading north to Smeaton Junction. This last part also followed the route of the Buccleuch Tramway. The route parallels the A6094 known as Salters Road. To the left of the road is a stone wall which marks the eastern perimeter of Dalkeith Country Park, still owned by the Duke of Buccleuch and open to the public.

The Cowden, Cowdenfoot, Dalkeith and Smeaton Collieries and the extensive Smeaton Brick and Tile Works lay along the section north from the viaduct. Much of this section of the trackbed has become part of the Penicuik to Musselburgh Foot and Cycleway and access to the trackbed is through the grounds of the newly-built shared campus of Dalkeith and St David's High Schools. A public footpath through the school grounds leads to the trackbed to Smeaton. This stretch of trackbed was once dominated by the Dalkeith Colliery, with its coal washing and screening plant, which was located at Smeaton Head, half-a-mile north of the industrial estate. The approach to Smeaton Junction, where the East Lothian lines to Macmerry and Gifford branched off, is dominated by overhead power lines and their supporting pylons. The industrial scars may have barely healed but the contrast with the opulence of Dalkeith Country Park to the left and the wooded hilltop of Carberry Tower to the north-east remains.

Smeaton Station (354694) was slightly to the north of Smeaton Junction. The station was located south of a minor road where the railway passed under a double-arched bridge. Before the bridge was an island platform, once overlooked on the right by a large brick signal box extended so that it overhung the original base. Exposed linkages and cabling ran from the signal box down a steep slope to the railway tracks. Steps led up from the short island platform to the road. The steps have been removed and the entrance from the road blocked off; the lighter coloured stone contrasting with the blackened stone of the rest of the bridge. The main station buildings were on the wide island platform with a large stone water tower topped by a metal tank to the south of the platform. No passenger service ever operated between Smeaton and Dalkeith despite assurances given to the contrary when the line was proposed. Passengers could use the station to travel to Edinburgh or east towards Macmerry or Gifford. The passengers on the line would have been confronted with sidings, on both sides, filled with coal wagons serving Dalkeith and Carberry Collieries.

Smeaton to Monktonhall Junction

From the road bridge at Smeaton station, the railway was carried on a high embankment which dominated the mining village of Whitecraigs to the left and the miners' cottages at Deanstown to the right of the trackbed. The miners' rows at Deanstown have been demolished and the village consigned to history. A mineral line from Carberry Colliery and Deans Pit fed into the railway three quarters of a mile north of Smeaton Station. The line crossed over the A6124 Musselburgh to Pathhead road to reach the Deans Pit and continued thereafter to the Carberry

Smeaton Station looking south towards the NCB coal washer

Colliery located on the northern edge of Carberry Hill. Gradients were severe (1 in 33 at worst) but output was half a million tons in 1906 with 750 men working in shifts. The colliery at Carberry eventually closed in 1960.

Carberry Tower, on the wooded slopes of Carberry Hill, was formerly run by the Church of Scotland but is now a Christian leadership training and conference centre. Carberry Hill was the site of a battle in 1567 between the armies of Mary Queen of Scots and nobles opposed to her. The tower which was converted into a mansion in 1819 dates from the sixteenth century.

The trackbed now stops abruptly, truncated by a road at the northern edge of Whitecraigs. A path winds down to the road. The rest of the trackbed has been removed with the Penicuik, Musselburgh Foot and Cycleway taking the road to the left and following the east bank of the River Esk to reach Musselburgh. The railway originally continued north towards the ECML joining it at Monktonhall Junction to the east of the River Esk and south of Musselburgh. Coal production from the Lothian coalfields increased dramatically before the First World War as did the profits. Serious proposals, sponsored by the mine-owners, were put forward to construct the series of tracks mentioned earlier and known as the Lothian Lines which would have duplicated most of the lines around Smeaton Station and improved access to the port of Leith. The North British managed to block those proposals and eventually provided more track to reduce the bottleneck at Leith port. As a consequence, the line between Monktonhall Junction and Smeaton Junction was doubled in December 1912.

The line between Smeaton Junction and Hardengreen Junction failed to thrive and it never realised its potential as a through connection to the Waverley route.

Cairntow level crossing and Jardine's cast iron bridge (see page 45)

A passenger service, also part of the original proposals, never materialised. Given the number of coal mines accessed by the lines, the failure to thrive is surprising but by the turn of the century the only traffic being generated was by Dalkeith Gas Works and the telegraph pole depot at Gibraltar sidings. The plans to construct the Lothian lines originally proposed to double this section and allow coal traffic from Newtongrange to travel along this route but like many plans for this line, these never came to fruition.

By November 1934, the Smeaton to Hardengreen line was closed leaving only a half-mile siding at each end. At the Hardengreen end, the short section known as "the Hole" was used to position banking engines for the Waverley, Penicuik and Leadburn routes. The Smeaton end was used to store dilapidated wagons although in the 1950s a new mine at Cowdenfoot, near Thorneybank, meant that a half mile stretch was re-laid to serve it.

With the decline of the coalfields and the closure of the branch lines to Macmerry and Gifford, the Monktonhall to Smeaton line was singled in 1973 and closed at the end of December 1980.

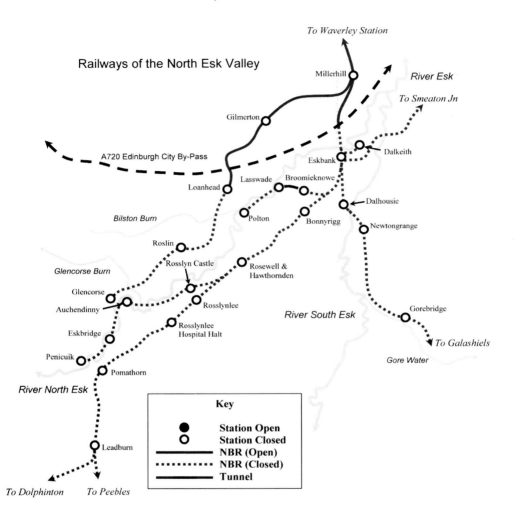

Railways of the North Esk Valley

Key

- ● Station Open
- ○ Station Closed
- ▬ NBR (Open)
- ▪▪▪ NBR (Closed)
- ▬ Tunnel

Chapter 3

The Railways of the North Esk Valley

The main attraction to the railway builders in the North Esk Valley was the Midlothian or Esk Basin coalfield and the outcropping of ironstone deposits which could supply the iron and steel manufacturers of Lanarkshire. Paper manufacture which had made use of the fast flowing river system for many years provided additional business for the railways.

The deep gorges cut by the water of the River North Esk and its tributaries provided a considerable challenge for the railway builders. Four railways were built as branches west from the Waverley Route and only one, the Peebles Railway (PR), avoided the River North Esk and its tributaries and that at the cost of forcing the townsfolk of Penicuik to cross the river to reach the railway. The Edinburgh, Loanhead and Roslin Railway (ELRR) stayed to the north of the River North Esk but it was still forced to cross Bilston Burn, a tributary, in grand style by the Bilston Glen viaduct. Frequent crossings of the river meant heavy engineering costs.

After much jockeying over possible routes by different local railway companies and plans by the Caledonian Railway (CR), the North British Railway (NBR) again reigned supreme, gaining control and operating the routes for the benefit of their shareholders. The first branch to be built was the PR in 1855 which eventually was extended along the Tweed Valley, forming a long loop which left the Waverley Route at Hardengreen Junction, near Eskbank in Midlothian and rejoined the Waverley Route in the Borders at Galashiels. The one and a half mile Esk Valley Railway (EVR), which opened in 1864, left the PR just west of Hardengreen Junction and the four and a half mile Penicuik Railway (PkR), which opened in 1872, branched west of Rosewell and Hawthornden Station. The Leadburn, Linton and Dolphinton Railway, opened in 1864, also branched from the PR but apart from the first few hundred yards near Leadburn, the branch ran through the Borders and is not included in this book. Finally in 1874, the Edinburgh, Loanhead and Roslin Railway was opened. It left the Waverley Route at Millerhill Junction, located between Edinburgh and Dalkeith, extended through Loanhead to Roslin and eventually, in 1877, reached the outskirts of Penicuik near Glencorse.

The branch line to Peebles was independent from its opening in 1855 until taken over by the NBR six years later. The journey between Eskbank, the nearest station on the Waverley Route, and Peebles took an hour and there were initially three trains each day. It passed through the mining communities of Bonnyrigg and Rosewell before curving south-west towards Penicuik but only reached the eastern bank of the gorge formed by the North Esk; near but not close enough to be of great value to the people of Penicuik who remained on the other side of this natural barrier and required the use of a horse bus to link the station with the town.

The railway then climbed south towards the 950 foot summit just south of Leadburn from where it headed down the Eddleston Valley towards Peebles, a distance of eighteen and three quarter miles from Eskbank. Costs were reduced by the choice of route with level crossings being a feature instead of bridges. The route was extended along the Tweed Valley, almost doubling the length, before eventually rejoining the Waverley Route near Galashiels by 1864. The Peebles loop contained some outstanding scenic beauty along with scenes of grim industrial mining life.

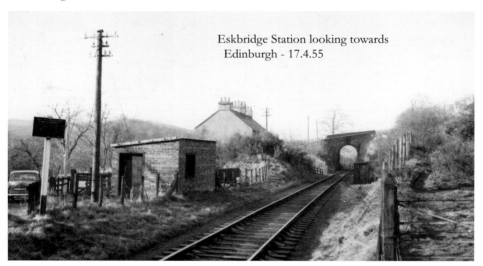

Eskbridge Station looking towards Edinburgh - 17.4.55

Not often does a railway have three birthdays but that is the distinction held by the EVR which started life as an independent railway company. The opening day was set for the first of April 1864 but the NBR using its muscle, since they provided the motive power, would not work the line because no station had been provided for Lasswade. The EVR sought arbitration and the NBR magnanimously agreed to work the line from the 15th April but in a twist, only understood by accountants, set the official opening for the 8th April even though no trains ran for the first week! The ruling about having a station at Lasswade eventually went against the EVR and it was built and opened just over four years later at a heavy cost to the company's profits, so tight were the margins involved in running a short local branch railway. The financial burden of this extra station reduced the dividend and made the EVR more vulnerable to takeover. The NBR duly obliged in 1871.

The EVR opened nine years after the opening of the Peebles. It was a heavily engineered line branching from the PR at the Esk Valley Junction in Bonnyrigg before cutting through high ground towards the steep-sided valley of the North Esk. It finally approached the deep river valley by a long tunnel before crossing the river twice as the railway descended towards the valley bottom to reach the terminus at Polton. Construction took nearly three years with some of the delay caused by opposition from the CR who were also considering the potential of a route into the Penicuik area.

The PkR followed the River North Esk for its entire length clinging first to the slopes of the historic Roslin Glen before turning sharply south still entwined with the river on the western slopes of Penicuik. The ELRR opened in July 1874 and was extended to Glencorse three years later. It was the last of the railways to be built in the valley of the North Esk and the final branch to extend from the Waverley Route in the Lothians. Passenger services, once running at five trains a day through to Edinburgh with an extra two at weekends, were an early casualty, the service stopping in 1933. Despite this, the Glencorse Railway was the last to close because of the rich returns from the many coal mines along the route. The line finally closed in 1991 having been briefly re-opened to take the remaining coal stocks from Bilston Glen Colliery to Cockenzie Power Station. Even today some of the rails remain in place.

Exploring the Railway Heritage

All the routes in this chapter are covered by the following maps;
Landranger 66; Explorer 344, 350

The Peebles branch from Hardengreen Junction to Leadburn and the Penicuik Railway

The route from Hardengreen Junction to Hawthornden Junction and on to Penicuik has been preserved as part of the Penicuik and Musselburgh Foot and Cycleway, although the first section from the junction to the west side of the A7 has been removed requiring a short detour. Between Hawthornden Junction and Leadburn, the trackbed of the PR exists only in sections and some stretches are difficult to trace. However, the exploration of the branch to Penicuik with its twists and frequent crossings of the River North Esk more than compensates for the loss of the trackbed. From Penicuik, it is possible to cross the River North Esk by road to reach the site of Pomathorn Station and complete a circuit north-east along the trackbed of the former PR back to Hawthornden Junction. It is also possible to explore this section in the reverse direction. The trackbed of the PR, south of Pomathorn, can also be explored to Leadburn where the former railway reaches the Scottish Borders.

There were stations on the Peebles Railway at Bonnyrigg (1.4 miles from Hardengreen Junction), Rosewell (3.3 miles), Rosslynlee (4.6 miles) and Pomathorn (6.8 miles). On the Penicuik Branch, there were stations at Rosslyn Castle (4.6 miles from Hardengreen Junction), Auchendinny (6 miles), Esk Bridge (7 miles) and Penicuik (7.7 miles).

Hardengreen Junction

The railway to Leadburn began at Hardengreen Junction (324662) climbing 750 feet in nine and a quarter miles. The site of Hardengreen Junction was located just south of the A6094 (Bonnyrigg Road) where the trackbed of the Waverley Route, at present a walkway, can be found.

At the start of the branch line, a coal lye held contractor's coal. The climb away from the junction was 1 in 53 and this led to an accident when wagons loaded with rails were allowed to run down the gradient towards the junction by gravity. The signalman had forgotten to reset the points to allow the wagons to run into the coal lye and the wagons emptied their contents over the junction and blocked it. Thereafter, the practice of allowing the train to descend by gravity was stopped. A further incident occurred at the same site when John Latta, a shoemaker by trade, who worked in the signal box, was allowed to continue to make shoes when there were no train movements. This arrangement worked well for eighteen years and in return, the railway company only paid him a part-time wage. Their economy

64

backfired when he was distracted by his shoemaking and forgot to free a hasp from the switch which was still set for the coal lye. The first passenger train of the day, en route to Eskbank, was derailed and the locomotive superintendent, the driver and two passengers were injured. It's not known what happened to John Latta but at least he had another trade to fall back on!

South of the junction site, the walkway continues behind a Tesco Store. A sign-posted path links the former Waverley Route with a pedestrian footbridge over the A7 which has been realigned to the west. On the west side of the bridge, the trackbed of the PR crosses a stretch of empty land before reaching the outskirts of Bonnyrigg and Lasswade. To the right of the former line at the start of playing fields, the EVR branched (318656). Views south towards the Moorfoot Hills are expansive and contrast with the council estates to the right. New housing in the aptly named Waverley Court is built along the trackbed on the approach to Bonnyrigg Station. Almost one and a half miles from Hardengreen Junction, the trackbed crossed Dundas Street by a level crossing and on the west side is the site of Bonnyrigg Station (312659) about a quarter of a mile south of the centre of the village. Opened in 1855 along with the PR, it was re-named Bonnyrigg Road in 1866, for two years when the EVR began operations and Broomieknowe Station was known as Bonnyrigg. The station buildings, originally of grey stone, have been demolished and the footbridge removed but the landscaped platforms form a link with the past. To the south and connected to the railway by a siding, was Polton Colliery Number 2.

The line continues west, eventually reaching open fields to the south beyond Sherwood Crescent and gradually closing with Rosewell Road. The remains of a platelayers hut still exist, its concrete construction suggesting it was erected after the reorganisation of the railways in 1923. There was a level crossing at Dalhousie Chesters where a farm road crossed the line. To the south of the line at this point was the Dalhousie Siding which served local farms. There are dog kennels a short distance further on before the trackbed passes under a road bridge which carried the original road into Rosewell prior to the construction of the bypass. To the south of the line, at this point, was a short branch to Dalhousie Sand quarry. The realignment of the A6094 means that Rosewell, the next mining community on the route, is now bypassed.

After the road bridge over the line, the trackbed passes to the north of a cemetery. Hawthornden Station (289632) was located next to the cemetery. The platforms again survive. Changes to station names on the Peebles line were common and the station was re-named Rosewell and Hawthornden in 1928. In 1962, the railway beyond Rosewell and Hawthornden, on the PR, was closed to passenger traffic but the remaining stump was used for freight traffic until 1967 when the Penicuik branch also lost its freight service. The bypass cuts across the line of the trackbed and the former railway can be located at a car park where the PkR starts. Hawthornden Junction has disappeared and the next section of trackbed towards Leadburn has been absorbed into a large field. Trailing in from the south-east at the junction was the mineral line from Whitehill Colliery and brickworks, all signs of which have been removed. From the junction, the Peebles railway crossed a more rural landscape.

Penicuik Railway

The path that leaves the car park (285639) follows the trackbed of the PkR. Two years in construction, the line opened in May 1872 for freight and then in September for passengers. In addition to the paper and coal industries, the railway company wanted to develop Penicuik as a dormitory town for Edinburgh hoping that those who could afford it would commute to the city.

The trackbed soon reaches wooded land as it approaches Roslin Glen and Roslin Glen Country Park, passing under several brick-lined overbridges en route. It required careful planning to establish a route on the south side of the steep gorge of the River North Esk and the trees mask the extent of the engineering required as a ledge had to be cut on the wooded hillside to carry the line.

Rosslyn Castle Station (273622) is located three quarters of a mile from Hawthornden Junction, at the overbridge carrying a minor road over the trackbed in an attractive wooded embankment. A single platform to the north side remains with steps leading up to the road and on the opposite side at the base of the overbridge is a red painted concrete plinth with Rosslyn Castle station picked out

in white stones. It was re-named from simply Rosslyn in 1872 to avoid confusion when the ELRR opened its Roslin Station in Roslin village on the opposite side of the North Esk gorge. Up the steps, beside the former station cottage, a twisting minor road quickly descends into the gorge and eventually crosses the river with views of Roslin Castle and the village of Roslin.

Eleven years before the battle of Bannockburn, a Scottish army, outnumbered almost four to one, faced an English army on the slopes of the gorge which formed a natural defence line. The English contrived to lose their numerical advantage by advancing their troops in three separate divisions. The first division was surrounded at night and defeated on the southern slopes of the glen. The next two English divisions advanced to the north of the glen where the major part of the battle was fought. They were repulsed by a Scottish army who knew the landscape and used it to their advantage. The memorial cairn for the battle of Roslin is located next to the Glencorse railway. Roslin Castle was built after the battle but was destroyed by fire in 1447 when a maid-servant lit a candle to search under a bed for a family pet. A century later, an English army of Henry VIII succeeded in destroying it as part of the 'rough wooing' of Mary Queen of Scots already mentioned in the chapter about Haddington. Having been rebuilt, it was captured in 1650 by a division of Cromwell's army led by General Monk.

West from the station site, the trackbed continues in a tree-lined cutting. There are signs of sidings overlooked by Lea Farm which may have provided links to a nearby quarry and pits; all now closed. At the bottom of the gorge where the road crosses the river, a gun powder mill, the first in the country, was opened in 1804 supplying gunpowder for use in the Napoleonic Wars. It was a good position for the mill since it was able to use the power of the river to mill the powder, wood from the slopes of the gorge to produce charcoal (an important ingredient in

10 arch Woodhouselee Viaduct between Rosslyn Castle Station and Auchendinny - Penicuik railway

Auchendinny Station looking towards
Edinburgh - 17.4.55

gunpowder manufacture) and any accidental explosions were confined in the gorge. It remained in business until 1954.

The fear of labouring steam trains producing a spark to ignite the works resulted in a most unusual structure known as the 'tin tunnel' being built. It was basically a covering over the line giving protection for the factory for all of 248 yards and was made of iron and timber. The 'tin tunnel' has been dismantled but an overbridge carrying a water pipeline from Gladhouse Reservoir, situated in the Moorfoot Hills, to Edinburgh still crosses the line. At this point, the trackbed is still located on a ledge cut out of the valley side which allows views of the river snaking across the fields of the valley floor but it soon crosses the twisting river seven times in just over two miles. The first crossing, the curved ten-arch Woodhouselee Viaduct (254617) is certainly the most spectacular. It is a category B listed structure of stone and brick and at its highest, offers dramatic views along the valley. To the left, the river does a 'U-turn' before disappearing into a narrow steep sided sandstone gorge crossed by a private road bridge. Some of the original railway railings remain on the parapets of the viaduct although they have been largely replaced by a more secure fence. The last arch crosses a minor road. The ruins of Old Woodhouselee Castle are in the trees on the hillside to the left of the trackbed just beyond the viaduct. As a young man, Sir Walter Scott practised his storytelling skills here, no doubt drawing inspiration from the dramatic setting which in his days did not include the railway. The remains of the castle overlook a sharp drop to the river at a bend in the gorge where the walls are unstable and are best avoided.

The trackbed quickly enters the 111 yard Firth Tunnel named after the nearby Firth House which is reached by a private bridge over the gorge. It emerges at the site of the Curtis Fine Paper Mill which was formerly known as the Dalmore Mill.

To the left are the steep red sandstone walls of the gorge as the river twists back towards the railway. The paper mill has encroached on the trackbed leaving only a narrow path which crosses Glencorse Burn, a tributary of the River North Esk, by a girder bridge. Beyond the access road to the mill is the 74 yard Auchendinny tunnel which passes under the narrow B7026 to emerge at a bowstring bridge over the North Esk. On a site restricted by the river, the curving platform of Auchendinny Station (252608), remains. The station buildings, signal box, crane and loading bay have been removed although the stationmaster's cottage is now a private residence. The signal box was perched on the narrow ridge between the railway and the river and must have been a great place to cast a fishing line! A stone retaining wall was built to stop the river eroding the site.

The trackbed again follows the river south towards Penicuik. Glencorse Barracks, originally known as Greenlaw Barracks, are on the far side of the river but out of sight at the top of a very steep bank cut by the river. The original terminus of the ELRR was beside Glencorse Barracks separated only by the width of the narrow river valley. The barracks area was originally the site of what would have been one of the largest prisoner of war camps in Britain if the Napoleonic Wars had not ended before construction was complete.

The trackbed cuts through fields, as the river valley widens again, before re-crossing the river by the Beeslack girder bridge. Industrial buildings, some closed, crowd in on the trackbed. A new bridge constructed as part of the pathway is also used by trucks to reach the sewage works to the left of the trackbed. The Harper's Brae sidings were in this area. The steep gorge walls are tree-lined and to the right, high above, is the town of Penicuik. Stone retaining walls were required along this stretch. The railway passed under a road which descends Harper's Brae, emerging beside the same steeply twisting road before it crossed over the river. Where the road turns sharp right to cross over the bridge, sat the cramped Eskbridge Station (246605), no trace of which remains. It opened in July 1874, closed as part of wartime economies between 1917 and 1919, and finally closed in 1930 since it lacked freight facilities and was in a poor position. Near the station were the Esk Mills which had their own sidings. Originally a cotton mill, it was used as a prisoner-of-war camp in Napoleonic times until a large breakout forced the government to move the camp further up the valley to Valleyfield.

The final part of the railway was closely entwined with the vast Valleyfield Paper Mills which was founded in 1708 and expanded over time before closing in July 1975. Many of the paper mill buildings, supported by concrete pillars, extend over the river which was twice more forced under the trackbed. The station at Penicuik (238598) had a single platform with a single storey station building and was dominated by the paper mill and a tall circular brick chimney. Beyond the station was a brick goods shed. The station was awkwardly placed at the bottom of the valley and a steep climb was required to reach the centre of Penicuik. Houses now occupy the station site.

The A701 crosses the river just beyond the station site. The passenger service was withdrawn in 1951 but freight services continued until 1967. Extensive house building now covers the former station and paper mill sites. Rarely can a railway have been so intimately entwined with a single river or have had such a concentration of engineering works to ensure the railway's safe passage. The fact that the trackbed has been so well-preserved ensures a fitting and lasting tribute to the railway builders. The residents of Penicuik must long for the railway to return to ease the pressure on the roads between the town and Edinburgh.

Penicuik Station from deadend - 10.6.50

Pomathorn

For the fit and adventurous, the exploration of the local railways can be continued by turning left on to the A701 and then taking first left. The inevitably steep gradient of Castle Brae (B6372) climbs the valley side towards Pomathorn where the former railway station is located next to mill buildings now used for storage. The PR can be traced from Pomathorn south to Leadburn or by turning north-east, the circuit back to the car park near Hawthornden Junction can be completed.

Towards Leadburn

South from Pomathorn Station site (243593) , the former railway headed towards the summit at Leadburn, crossing the B6372 by another level crossing. The trackbed snakes across the open moorland to reach the only substantial engineering works on the Peebles branch which were required to cross the Lead Burn west of the small village of Howgate. The brick abutments with wing walls and two piers are all that remain of the bridge. Most days the burn is not difficult to cross. There are now extensive views west towards the Pentlands and as far as Tinto Hill in Lanarkshire, a measure of how far the railway has climbed. The trackbed continues through woods then over a minor bridge alongside a small reservoir and passes a row of cottages before reaching the site of another level crossing at Venture Fair. The last stretch of track before Leadburn is on the slopes of the Lead Burn valley. A narrow field for horses has claimed some of the trackbed before a final brick bridge and the approach to the A6094.

The railway cut across the road at an angle, over another level crossing, before it reached Leadburn Station (235555) which closed in 1955. By that time, the Dolphinton line had already closed. The station site has been preserved as a picnic area and there are swings between the platforms. Here, on the boundary with the Scottish Borders, the views in all directions make the stop worthwhile. The small hamlet is situated at a crossroads where roads cross into Midlothian and south to the Borders and west to Lanarkshire.

Towards Hawthornden Junction

Originally known as Penicuik until that town got its own station down in the valley, Pomathorn Station was extended when the NBR took over the line. That company built a brick building with an overhanging canopy at right angles to the original stone station building which the PR had built. The NBR's brick extension appears to have been demolished but the original building is now a private residence. Eventually the station became an unmanned halt before closing in 1962.

The trackbed then runs north-east and looks across to Penicuik on the other side of the valley. It then crosses a road at another level crossing where a railway cottage still remains. To the east of the road, the trackbed runs in a shallow cutting towards woods. There is a missing bridge before a further level crossing near Firth Mains. Near Rosslynlee Hospital, the conditions become dreadful with no easy path. The trackbed, while discernible through the woods, has been blocked by fallen trees and is very overgrown. In the woods was the short-lived Rosslynlee Hospital Halt (268613) which served the nearby hospital. It only opened in December 1958 and

71

was an attempt to encourage the use of the new diesel trains but was closed in February 1962 when the Peebles line closed.

Beyond the hospital, conditions improve but only marginally because the drainage has been ruined by a pipeline laid after the route closed. The last station before Hawthornden Junction was Rosslynlee Station (274618), a remote outpost with only farms around it. Originally named Roslin in an attempt to link it with Roslin village about two miles away, the NBR insisted that the name be changed to either Gourlaw or Rosslynlee, the names of two local farms, and the PR chose the latter. The station building constructed by the PR with the NBR extension and platform at right angles, is used as a private residence.

The trackbed continues beyond the station to the edge of a large field looking towards the car park at the start of the Penicuik railway walk. At this point, the trackbed has reverted to agricultural use and a detour around the field is required. Given that it was a lightly engineered route, it is perhaps not surprising that parts of the trackbed have suffered badly over time.

Esk Valley Railway

Only two sections of the railway can be traced. The first section is where the EVR branched from the Peebles branch up to Bonnyrigg High Street. The tunnel, located to the west of the High Street, is sealed at both portals. The Lasswade Viaduct is also blocked at both ends and the second bridge over the River North Esk has been demolished. The section on the valley floor from the site of Polton Station to the demolished railway bridge can be traced as can the short section between the two railway bridges. There were stations at Broomieknowe (0.5 mile from Esk Valley Junction), Lasswade (1 mile) and Polton (1.5miles)

The communities connected by the railway are extremely close together. Bonnyrigg and Lasswade are cheek by jowl on the high ground above the valley with Polton in the valley floor of the North Esk. From Esk Valley Junction (318656), the line almost immediately entered a deep cutting for the first half-mile, passing under Lothian Road, before reaching the site of Broomieknowe Station (308656) which was called Bonnyrigg until 1868. The original name was not surprising given that the railway passed through the Eldindean and Quarryhead districts of Bonnyrigg. This section is preserved as a broad walkway with distant views back towards the Moorfoot hills and Midlothian mining communities such as Newtongrange. Located next to what is now a children's play park, the station, with its single platform and waiting room, has disappeared since the cutting has been partially filled in.

Beyond Broomieknowe Station, the railway passed under Bonnyrigg High Street and then descended into an even deeper cutting before reaching the portal of the 430 yard Lasswade tunnel. Both portals of the tunnel are sealed and the section is not worth exploring. A detour is required to reach the other side of the tunnel and can be made by following the High Street north-west to the Wee Brae to reach Polton Road and then turning right into Elm Row. Elm Row leads to the river and the last road on the left before the river is Westmill Road which, if followed to the end, takes you to the site of Lasswade Station and the viaduct over the River North Esk. A housing estate occupies the site but the western portal of the sealed-off and uninviting tunnel is visible. Lasswade Station (303657) consisted of a simple brick building on a short platform on a curve in the line and a piece of this platform still straddles the portal of the tunnel.

Leaving the gloom of the station site, the railway reached the river and the six-arch stone Polton Viaduct (301657) which is category B listed and fenced off. Once over the river, the railway began a rapid descent towards the next crossing; this time by a simpler single pier, metal sided bridge. This section can be accessed from the A768 Wadingburn Road and turning left on to Kevock Road. The road descends quickly into the valley, twisting and turning before reaching a riding centre. The abutment of a missing bridge indicates the line of the railway. Before the Glencorse railway opened, ironstone and coal for the Shotts Iron Company was carted down to the Kevock Sidings from the Mauricewood Pits near Penicuik. This business was lost to the ELRR despite the EVR offering generous rebates.

To reach the site of Polton Station (289649) means tracing the route back to Polton Road and following the twisting Polton Bank road to the valley floor. The station site was next to the road bridge over the river and is now occupied by a housing estate. Around the terminus of the railway were two important paper mills; the Polton Paper Mill and, to the south of the road, the Springfield Paper Mill. The fast-flowing River North Esk provided the power and the railway provided the means of taking away the finished rolls of paper. Both paper mills were founded in the mid-eighteenth century. The route of the railway can be traced back to the missing rail bridge. The trackbed is now used to exercise horses which can cross the river from the riding school next to the site of the Kevock Sidings.

Another source of potential income was the development of the EVR as a suburban route serving Edinburgh since for many it provided the only realistic way of reaching that city. In 1910, there were ten return journeys between the city and the stations on the branch but this had reduced by half when passenger services were withdrawn in 1951. The branch closed completely in 1964.

The Glencorse Branch

What remains of this railway is linked to the closing dates of the different sections. Most traces of the Roslin to Glencorse section which was the earliest to close, in 1959, have been removed. In 1969, the short section between Roslin and Bilston Glen Colliery was closed including the viaduct over the Bilston Burn. In 1999, the viaduct was re-opened as part of a walkway with the help of Midlothian Council and the Edinburgh Green Belt Trust who brought together many different interested parties and sources of funding. There was a plan to lift the track between Loanhead Station and Millerhill and move it to Ayrshire but the cost of doing so could not be justified and the rails remain in situ although very overgrown. Most of the trackbed has been taken over by Sustrans so there is little chance of it ever re-opening although the rails were left in place when a bridge was constructed over the trackbed during the building of the Edinburgh bypass. The only section worth walking is between Loanhead Station and Roslin.

The ELRR left the line at Millerhill Junction and had stations at Gilmerton (2.75 miles from Millerhill Junction), Loanhead (4.25 miles), Roslin (6 miles) and Glencorse (8 miles). The branch was extended to service the Penicuik Gas Works. Overlooked to the west by the Pentland Hills, the route climbed from Millerhill Junction to the Gas Works with little respite. The branch had an interesting history with several sidings steeped in industrial heritage including the Straiton Sidings which served the shale oil industry and limekilns at Burdiehouse with links to Bilston Glen and Roslin collieries amongst others. At times, the Glencorse branch ran very close to both the Polton branch just down the road from Loanhead and the Penicuik branch just across the River North Esk near Glencorse Barracks.

Millerhill Junction

There had been a station at Millerhill since the opening of the Waverley Route but alterations were made when the ELRR opened. The station was located immediately to the south of the B6415 and to the west of it were the Edmonstone Iron Works. Apart from a gap being created by the construction of a pipeline across a section of embankment near Millerhill, the rails remain in place as far as Loanhead Station. The trackbed leaves Millerhill Junction (327695) through a cutting which swings south-west to pass under the A6106, Millerhill Road before reaching open countryside near the Kaim overbridge. This overbridge marks the limit of the track owned by the railway authorities. The rest of the route, including the section with the rails still in situ, is owned by Sustrans.

The trackbed continues to climb slowly, crossing over the A7 (Old Dalkeith Road) then underneath the A772 to the Gilmerton Station site (297680) which when open was overlooked by Gilmerton Colliery. From here, the track crossed over the Lasswade Road by a low bridge. Having been struck on more than one occasion by road traffic, it had to be raised and double deck buses can now pass under it for the first time. The trackbed then runs parallel to the Edinburgh by-pass before passing underneath it.

Straiton Sidings

The rails are still in place between the by-pass and Loanhead Station but in many places, the trackbed is very overgrown and not easy to walk. There is also a feeling of unease about walking where there are rails even though the extent of foliage would make it impossible for a train to get far without being de-railed.

South of the by-pass, the trackbed divides an industrial scrapyard to the east from the site of the Straiton Sidings. These extensive sidings which left the railway on a rising gradient served the Straiton limeworks and reached north to Burdiehouse and south west to Pentland to connect to the local oil shale and limestone industries. Already in existence when the line opened, shale oil production struggled under different ownerships. The Clippens Oil Company established in Paisley and seeking new sources of shale oil, took over in 1881. It initially used the railway to transfer stock to their main depot in Paisley but eventually concentrated refining at Straiton. Although the operation was plagued by fires, floods, strikes and competition from abroad, it was the new water supply to Edinburgh which finally closed it down. Two underground aqueducts carrying the supply gave the water company rights to minerals for 40 yards around the pipes and when Clippens Oil encroached on this area, the Water Company exercised these rights and production was halted after a protracted legal dispute. The mining operation at one time employed around 500 miners. Limestone production was also associated with the area and there were kilns at Burdiehouse. Production ebbed and flowed and even saw new track laid in the mid-sixties but this was never used and the facility was demolished about that time.

A retail park has been built on the site of the Straiton limeworks and some of the shale pits, which had caused the ground to subside, were used as a landfill site. The part of the sidings which stretches from the former trackbed of the ELRR west to the site of the retail park have been retained as a path to give access to Straiton Pond Nature Reserve. The pond was formed from the remains of a blue clay quarry. At the entrance to the nature reserve from the west side was the level crossing which crossed the B702. The series of sidings continued beyond this level crossing with a branch north towards Burdiehouse and Mortonhall pits and lime works. The line also continued southward, with various sidings reaching different parts of the Straiton Oil Works, before eventually running parallel to the A701 and turning sharply west to cross the road to the Pentland Oil Works. South of the Straiton Sidings, the trackbed curves to the left and passes the Eldin Chemical Works, now an industrial estate, which was served by a siding. To the west are several tall grain silos, before the trackbed passes under a cast iron overbridge which carries Edgefield Road. The section of trackbed from the Edgefield overbridge is considerably overgrown and is only for the dedicated enthusiast.

South of the overbridge, to the left, the northern approach to the Ramsey Colliery which once dominated the land to the west was controlled by the demolished Edgefield Weighs Signal Box. The trackbed swung south-west around the colliery before reaching Loanhead Station where it was served by a series of sidings to the west of the track. Tree planting has helped to soften the scars left by the Ramsey Pit which dominated the town for so long. At the edge of the Midlothian coalfield, the coal with the seams at a steep angle, was for a long time difficult to extract but the 'Ramsey' was worked for over a hundred years and was named after an early owner. It was once owned by the Shotts Iron Company. A screening plant and a washer which also served other local pits was added in the nineteen twenties. Photographs of the pit show extensive sidings running parallel to the railway beside the station.

To the east of the track before the station were the premises of Mactaggart Scott. Their engineering skills are still used to design and construct marine hydraulic equipment. Prior to the Second World War, a siding was provided to allow the firm to remove its products by rail. Catapults for launching sea planes from warships was one of the more unusual products transported by the railway. Beyond this firm's extensive factories, also to the left, sits the goods shed, still intact and well-maintained, its wooden walls and hip-roofed structure belying its considerable age.

The station buildings (283657), by contrast, were more modest. A long low brick wall separated the extensive platform from the goods yard. The stationmaster's house was built in 1874 behind and at right angles to the original ticket office, now demolished. When a brick built extension was opened in 1894 with a canopy extending over the platform, a concourse was created. In time, the station was overlooked by the local primary school.

Immediately south of the station, Sustrans have laid a tarmac path along the former trackbed. The path is lit at night and has several access points as it passes through the centre of Loanhead after entering a stretch of deep cutting. The railway ran under the town's two principal streets; Clerk Street and The Loan. The bridge which carries Clerk Street is so wide, at 46 yards, that it just falls short by 7 yards

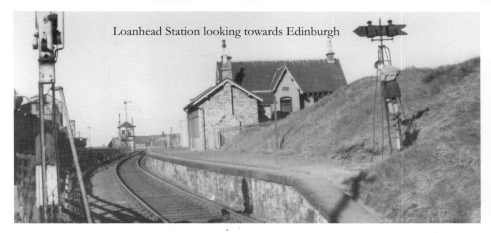

Loanhead Station looking towards Edinburgh

of being considered a tunnel! The next overbridge is skewed. The steep banks frequently require to be buttressed by stone retaining walls. The tree-lined cutting ends just short of the Bilston Glen Viaduct. To the left is a cemetery and to the right is a wide open space which once contained multiple sidings to serve Bilston Glen Colliery. Before the Bilston Glen sidings were opened, this was the location of the earlier Burghlee Colliery which was closer to the railway. The National Coal Board developed plans, originally proposed by the Shotts Iron Company who operated the Burghlee Colliery, to expand and exploit the coal reserves in

the area. The Burghlee Colliery closed in 1964 just after Bilston Glen Colliery was opened. From this site, coal trains were hauled continuously to Millerhill en route to Cockenzie Power Station. The removal of the pithead coal reserves at Bilston Glen provided the last traffic on the line and the colliery site is now an industrial estate.

Loanhead cutting today

Bilston Glen Viaduct

In some people's minds, historic monuments, castles and churches are considered to be more significant than industrial heritage. It is pleasing to note a change in this attitude and the restoration of the Bilston Glen Viaduct (281648) highlights the importance of preserving industrial monuments. Situated in a heavily wooded deep gorge, the viaduct which spans the Bilston Glen is a wonderful example of

Victorian engineering and is worthy of its Grade B listing. It consists of a single deep wrought iron span supported on low piers with a second pair of massive granite abutments at each end to support the line at high level. The central truss is 330 feet long by 40 feet deep with a 56 feet span at each end and was the biggest span of its type in Scotland. Strong concrete bases were constructed to support two new piers, each with granite coping to take the expansion bearings.

The present viaduct replaced an earlier viaduct which had been the source of a dispute with local colliery owners. The first viaduct was 498 feet in length supported on slender brick piers, 150 feet above the glen at its centre. Coal mining had caused subsidence to the original viaduct and a dispute arose as to how to strengthen the bridge. The problem was not with the brick piers but with the stone abutments which had settled slightly. Best practice was not to touch the coal within a certain radius of a viaduct but in the glen, coal working had encroached within 50 yards. The NBR wanted to replace the structure with an embankment but this was not acceptable to the landowner who deemed that this would forever spoil the scenic beauty of the glen through which the Bilston Burn, a tributary of the River North Esk, flows.

While a decision was being reached, the Shotts Iron Company could not be permitted to extract coal within 250 yards of the viaduct and were entitled to claim compensation. This changed the minds of the NBR and a replacement viaduct was decided on. Surprisingly, the original structure was dismantled and replaced with the present structure in only 11 days. A set of the expansion mountings, which were replaced when the viaduct was renovated, sit beside the viaduct. Ball bearings within the replacement mountings allowed the bridge to expand by two and a half inches on hot days. The decking has also been renewed and the parapets heightened for safety reasons. Now, everyone can enjoy a stroll across the viaduct to admire it and pause to appreciate the view down the valley towards Polton. It also helps to remind you of the difficult geography of the area with its deep gorges.

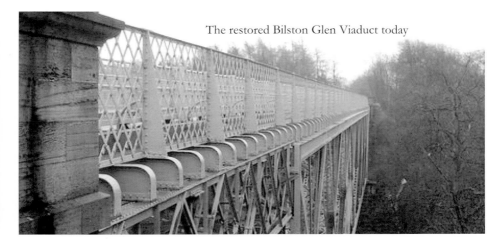

The restored Bilston Glen Viaduct today

Roslin

To the south of the viaduct, the trackbed initially passes through the Bilston Woods. There is a missing rail bridge (easily bypassed) and two overbridges on this stretch. The trackbed passes through the Dryden Mains estate. Located at the entrance to the estate is the memorial to the Battle of Roslin fought in this area on 24th of February 1303. The second of the three English divisions was overwhelmed here.

The trackbed runs parallel to the estate access road and then curves south-west towards Roslin passing to the rear of the famous Roslin Institute, home of Dolly, the first cloned sheep in the world, a symbol for life continuously re-created. In contrast, to the south-west of the Roslin Institute on the steep banks of Roslin Glen, stands Rosslyn Chapel. The chapel is a place of religious intrigue with its mysterious carvings of plants from the New World which predate Columbus's discovery of these lands by a hundred years and its connections with the Knights Templar and Freemasons. Rosslyn Chapel has recently become a world wide attraction due to its appearance in Dan Brown's best-selling book the 'Da Vinci Code'. Underneath the stone floors, there is believed to be a hidden vault with much speculation about its contents. It is strange that on either side of this modest mining village, separated by a disused railway trackbed, can be found such contrasting views of eternity; the scientific clone with the spiritual mystery.

In a section of cutting between Roslin and Bilston Glen Viaduct, to the rear of what is now the Roslin Bio Centre, a train from Glencorse was de-railed on a right hand curve. The engine was toppled, trapping and killing the fireman whilst the engine driver and several passengers were badly shaken. A large crowd gathered on hearing the news. An inquiry was quickly convened and exhaustive investigations struggled to reach a conclusion. In the end, it was thought that the train, aided by a falling gradient, was travelling too fast and that the engine was being operated in reverse suggesting that the turntable at Roslin Station was not in use at this time.

The approach to Roslin Station and the station site (273636) has been built on. The station burnt down in 1959. The station site had been purchased from the local school board. A detour through Roslin leads to the next overbridge which carries the B7006. The space under the bridge has been reduced in size and consists of a corrugated metal tube suitable for pedestrian use. The railway originally stopped at Roslin but was extended to Glencorse in 1877. A visit to Rosslyn Chapel is highly recommended. Beyond the bridge, the trackbed skirts a housing estate built after the railway was closed. The path veers to the right following the branch line to the Roslin Colliery. The trackbed of the ELRR is very overgrown until the Penicuik Road. Any signs of the colliery have been removed. Known locally as 'The Moat' after a local farm, it also worked some of the edge coals of the Lothian coalfield along with seams on the floor of the basin. The mine had a troubled beginning but with a new shaft sunk, access to better coal was achieved. Brick works briefly added to the local employment around the beginning of the Second World War with many of the bricks being used to construct air raid shelters.

The next two overbridges have been dismantled and a large sand quarry has removed all traces of the trackbed. A golf range and the alterations to the B7026 have also removed signs of the railway. Sadly, Glencorse Viaduct has also been removed. Built of local brick from nearby Whitehill Colliery at Rosewell, the fifteen semi-circular arches crossed the wide shallow valley of the River North Esk. Its brick construction eventually led to its demolition as bricks were falling from the viaduct on to the golf course below. The viaduct, which by this time was in the ownership of the golf club, was too expensive to maintain and was blown up. Surprisingly, the army who had a significant presence at nearby Glencorse barracks declined the offer to practise their skills with explosives.

From the viaduct, the trackbed on a rising gradient of 1 in 70 entered a cutting and passed under the Edinburgh to Penicuik road by another wide overbridge which again was just short of being classified as a tunnel. The end of the branch for passengers was at Glencorse Station (242615). Opposite Glencorse Barracks, the station was in the 'ELRR style' with a single long platform and the station master's house at right angles. The station site was cramped by a road to one side and a hillside to the other. There were two sidings. Coal was fed in from Greenlaw Colliery, on the hillside above the railway, which was redeveloped with the opening of the line. The name of the station was referred to in the original plans as Greenlaw but this would have caused confusion with Greenlaw Station on the Reston to St Boswells route in Berwickshire. The station was also referred to

Glencorse Viaduct (now demolished) looking towards Edinburgh - 11.8.63

as Glencross but this only lasted 3 months when a local resident who happened to be the Lord President of the Court of Session decided on Glencorse. Part of the station site is now a vehicle park for the barracks.

The railway extended beyond the station as a mineral line with sidings serving Mauricewood Colliery to the right and continuing across the Edinburgh to Penicuik road by a level crossing and then an underbridge to reach the site of the Penicuik Gasworks near Eastfield. The Shotts Iron Company had attempted to develop a pit at Eastfield but this was unsuccessful due to flooding. They did not wish to lose out on their investment and turned their attention to the nearby hillside to the west of the line where ironstone and coal deposits were known to exist at Mauricewood. The pit was opened before the extension was built and, for over a year, ironstone and coal had to be conveyed by road to the Kevock sidings on the Polton branch. The company also built a small community for miners and their families from other coalfields which became known as Shottstown. The Shottstown Miners Welfare and Social Club still exists although the houses were demolished in the nineteen- fifties. At Mauricewood, the coal production eventually became more prominent as ironstone production declined. When the Glencorse extension was opened in 1877, an incline at right angles to the railway was used to take coal down to the trackbed.

In September 1899, seventy men and boys were trapped when a fire broke out in the engine room at the pithead and fumes spread throughout the pit aided by an open ventilation door which should have been shut. Some bodies were recovered but the fires which still raged prevented others being reached until the following spring. After this, the pit was not worked continuously and closed in 1909. The Mauricewood disaster was the worst in the history of mining in the Lothian coalfield.

This last section of the trackbed has been built on with Mauricewood Primary School covering the trackbed to the north of the road and a supermarket covering the trackbed on the other side.

From beginning to end, this was a railway dominated by the existence of coal pits with each station being overlooked by pitheads. As the coal pits closed, there was no reason to keep the railway open and with the closure of Bilston Glen, in 1989, it was of no further use. The railways of the River North Esk have all been abandoned. The only one to survive the closure of the Waverley Route was the ELRR due to the importance of Bilston Glen Colliery and the fact that it branched from Millerhill yard which is now operated by the English, Welsh and Scottish Railway. Ironically, the demand for passenger services to Edinburgh, the least successful part of the railways when they were open, would be considerable today as the city experiences growth and pressure on both roads and housing. However, it is too late now for the Penicuik Express!

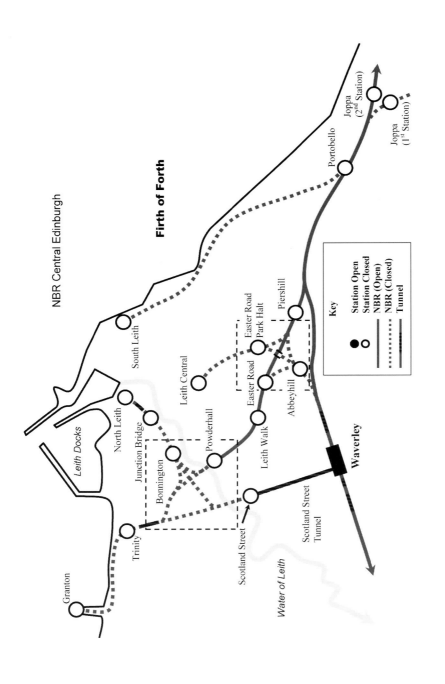

NBR Central Edinburgh

Firth of Forth

Leith Docks

Water of Leith

Granton
Trinity
North Leith
Junction Bridge
Bonnington
Powderhall
Scotland Street
Scotland Street Tunnel
Leith Central
Leith Walk
Easter Road
Easter Road Park Halt
Piershill
Abbeyhill
South Leith
Portobello
Joppa (2nd Station)
Joppa (1st Station)
Waverley

Key

Station Open
Station Closed
NBR (Open)
NBR (Closed)
Tunnel

Chapter 4

Edinburgh :
Suburban Lines to the North of the City

Before the Forth railway bridge was opened, the railway service between Edinburgh and the ports of Granton, Newhaven and Leith provided a vital link for both goods and people travelling north. From the three ports on the Forth, the journey north could be continued by a short ferry crossing to the nearby Fife coast avoiding a long detour west towards Kincardine.

When the railway era began, the trains passed through open countryside on their journey from Edinburgh to the three ports but by the time of their demise, they were part of the fabric of the large conurbation that is now the City of Edinburgh. The railways played an important role in the development of the present city with their links to the docks, local industry and the growing residential developments.

The North British Railway Company (NBR) established itself as the dominant force in railway building between Edinburgh and the Forth coast but it was soon joined in competition by its great rival, the Caledonian Railway (CR). These two companies who were wary of each others intentions provided saturation coverage of the area. They fought each other for diminishing revenues, ignoring the increasing threat of competition from buses and trams and deluding themselves into thinking that more trains or better facilities such as Leith Central Station were all that was needed. The same scenario was repeated all over Scotland and the failure of the lines built around the start of the twentieth century bear a bitter testimony to the lack of realistic forward planning and an inability to notice their true competitor - the bus.

In their defence, the railways in the north of the city were disadvantaged by the geography of the area. The cramped location of the main station at Waverley, wedged in a valley between the Castle Rock and the high ground of the New Town and Calton Hill, meant either building tunnels or creating longer routes by going east or west before looping around towards the ports. The blocking tactics of the rival railway companies and awkward landowners further restricted the choice of routes.

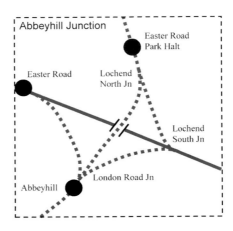

Abbeyhill Junction

Easter Road Park Halt

Easter Road

Lochend North Jn

Lochend South Jn

London Road Jn

Abbeyhill

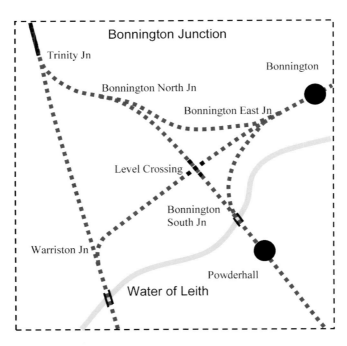

Bonnington Junction

Trinity Jn

Bonnington North Jn

Bonnington

Bonnington East Jn

Level Crossing

Bonnington South Jn

Warriston Jn

Powderhall

Water of Leith

A bold but impractical attempt to build a direct route to the coast by opening the Scotland Street tunnel under the New Town only highlighted the problems the railway builders faced. After taking over this direct route, the NBR soon closed the tunnel and opened branches that left the main line east of what became Waverley Station before turning towards Leith. The CR, frustrated in its attempts to make a connection at Haymarket Station and then through to Waverley Station, had also to reach Leith by a circuitous route from the west. These first routes were longer than the more direct routes offered by trams and buses and, in addition, the stations were often not in the best locations. The climb up the steps from Waverley Station to Princes Street cannot have helped when rival forms of transport could drop passengers off at street level.

In 1923, the railways underwent a major rationalisation with the NBR being absorbed into the London and North Eastern Railway (LNER) and the CR being absorbed into the London Midland and Scottish Railway (LMSR). The fact that so many lines survived this rationalisation and the nationalisation of the railways in 1948 suggests that the Edinburgh folk liked their railways but in the end they just didn't use them enough. With the city's present transport problems, maybe the lines were abandoned too quickly but due to the foresight of planners on the Council, Sustrans and SPOKES (The Lothian Cycle Campaign), most of the routes have been preserved as cycle paths that not only provide opportunities for recreation but preserve links with the railway era.

North British Railway Branches

The first railway to reach the Firth of Forth (in 1835) was the Edinburgh and Dalkeith Company's line from Portobello to South Leith Station on Constitution Street. Although the station closed in 1904 after Leith Central opened, most of this line survives as a freight line on the seaward side of Seafield Road. The journey east to Portobello from North Bridge, later Waverley Station, and north-west to Leith was too circuitous to be popular with the travelling public.

The Port of Leith which developed along the shores on each side of the estuary of the Water of Leith, was for a long time the most important port in Scotland. Ferries transported people and goods to the Fife coastline and beyond from Leith and the smaller ports of Newhaven and Granton which lay to the west. The connecting journey, by stagecoach, between Edinburgh and Leith was frequently slow and unreliable and in 1836 an Act of Parliament sanctioned the Edinburgh, Leith and Newhaven Railway which was intended to run from Princes Street Gardens through a long tunnel under the New Town to the coast at Newhaven with a branch to Leith. The proposals included a 1052 yard tunnel underneath the New Town from Princes Street to Scotland Street at a gradient of 1 in 27. The ambitious tunnel scheme involved burrowing beneath the foundations of the grand houses of the New Town which upset the residents and with awkward landowners at the Leith end of the branch, construction was slow. Additional opposition came from those who did not share the belief that a railway was likely to make a profit.

A further parliamentary act in 1839 retained the tunnel but modified the route to reach the coast at Trinity overlooking the shore and to the west of Newhaven. In 1842 the service between Canonmills Station (later Scotland Street) and Trinity Station began. The railway extended north from Canonmills through a short 148 yard tunnel under Rodney Street, crossed the Water of Leith by a bridge at Warriston before passing through a deep cutting and the 144 yard Trinity tunnel to reach the terminus at Trinity Station. The station was on high ground on the south side of Starbank Road, short of the shoreline at Newhaven, overlooking Chain Pier and station passengers had to walk down to the pier while goods had to be manhandled to the shoreline.

The Canonmills site was also awkwardly sited some distance from the city centre and the horse-drawn carriages provided stiff competition for the fledgling railway. It was intended to use steam locomotives on the line from Canonmills to Trinity but although tenders were invited, they were never ordered and horses had to provide the motive power. Trains were consistently late because of the gradients and the heavy coaches had to be replaced by lighter rolling stock.

Realising the limitations of the original terminus at Trinity, a further Act of Parliament was sanctioned in 1844, with a mile long extension across the shore road, west of Trinity, along the foreshore to a new harbour at Granton together with a branch from Warriston to Leith. The name of the railway was altered. in 1844, to the Edinburgh, Leith and Granton Railway (ELGR) to reflect the changed

Trinity Station looking north
8.11.81

location of the terminus. The harbour, built by the Duke of Buccleuch, was already operating a successful ferry service to Fife and the railway provided an important link when the Granton extension opened in 1846. The fortunes of the struggling line were transformed. The extension to Granton took the railway slightly west of the original terminus at Trinity with a new station being built at Trinity and a few months later, the branch to Leith was finally opened. This short one and a quarter mile branch left the Granton route at Warriston Junction, north of the railway bridge over the Water of Leith, and kept close to the north bank of the river before reaching Leith Docks.

The route was completed in 1847 when the missing link between the city centre and the coast was opened: the Scotland Street tunnel. The Princes Street terminus, at the southern end of the tunnel, was generally known as Canal Street but sometimes just as Princes Street and occupied part of the valley between the old and New Towns. The name Canal Street derived from an earlier abandoned scheme to extend the Union Canal through this area to Leith which never materialised. The station site was cramped and at a right angle to North Bridge Station, opened months before by the Edinburgh and Glasgow Railway. The EGR, after much opposition, had just extended their route from Haymarket Station. To add to the congestion at the site, the NBR's North Bridge Station, which opened almost a year earlier, was end on to the EGR station and the two companies co-operated to allow carriages to be transferred between the two routes. Each company had a separate booking office with the NBR booking office near North Bridge and the EGR's on Waverley Bridge.

Entrance to the Canal Street Station was either by the first floor of a two-storey building facing Princes Street or by a steep ramp to the tunnel entrance. Trains descended the slope through the tunnel with the assistance of a brake wagon attached to the front and ascending trains were pulled up to Canal Street by a stationary winding engine. There was a connection between the Edinburgh, Leith and Granton line and the Edinburgh and Glasgow line by means of a tightly-curved west facing spur which restricted the type of engine and carriage to four wheels.

With the route open to the coast and its prospects transformed, other companies started to court the ELGR and the EGR looked like being the successful suitors. Preliminary contracts were entered into but the plans fell through. In July 1847, the ELGR's short life ended when it was taken over by the Edinburgh and Northern Railway (ENR) which had just bought the Granton to Burntisland ferries and had a network of tracks throughout Fife extending to Perth and Dundee. The ENR quickly secured a monopoly on the Fife ferries putting the old ELGR line at the heart of railway activity. As railway companies grouped and re-grouped to gain territory and a share of lucrative markets, the Edinburgh & Northern became the Edinburgh, Perth and Dundee Railway (EPDR) in April 1849 and eventually part of the NBR portfolio at the end of July 1862. In February 1850, the EPDR introduced one of the world's first boat trains on the Granton to Burntisland crossing to carry goods wagons. Some believe it was the world's first boat train but that honour lies with a service in Northumberland.

EPDR passengers travelling from Edinburgh to Aberdeen still started their journey at Princes Street Gardens in the narrow confines of the tunnel, freewheeling to Scotland Street, before travelling along the branch to reach a ferry at Granton. By the time the NBR inherited this system, they realised that the spur, between the Scotland Street tunnel and the main line to what was now known as Waverley Station, was becoming too limiting as it could only cope with four-wheeled engines. The NBR was also facing competition from the newly opened CR branch to Granton and they needed to build an easier route to compete.

The solution was a new junction at Piershill almost two miles east of Waverley Station which was opened in 1868 and provided an alternative route to Trinity and Leith. From Piershill Junction, the route headed north-west from the main line crossing under Easter Road, Leith Walk and Ferry Road before joining the original route to Trinity south of Trinity tunnel. Two valuable connections were added which ensured that it was possible to run directly from Waverley to North Leith. The first was a short spur from what would become Easter Road Station to the mainline at Abbeyhill Junction passing under London Road and the second was from the new route to join the Scotland Street to Leith line at Bonnington which it crossed on the level. The line opened with one new station at Leith Walk and, in 1869, Abbeyhill Station was added on the short spur. In 1886, another short spur from Abbeyhill Station to the Piershill line was built, creating a minor loop to the East Coast mainline and completing a triangular junction between Abbeyhill Station and the Piershill line (London Road Junction). Other stations at Piershill and Easter Road opened during 1891 with a station at Powderhall opening in 1895. Powderhall was never busy especially when expected housing developments did not materialise and it didn't reopen after the First World War. Just west of Easter Road station, a spur gave access to the substantial Leith Walk East Goods, the site of which has now been built upon.

The new branch line veered from the main line at Piershill Junction located near the bottom of Restalrig Road South. This road eventually became better known as Smoky Brae and was well named because it was next to St Margarets Locomotive Shed, which was located on both sides of the East Coast Main Line (ECML), where the steep descent from Waverley Station had eased, and due to constant movement of steam engines loading up with coal at the coaling plant, was a smoky site. The residents of the nearby tenements could not open their windows such was the pollution and public health concerns remained throughout its life. Pollution was

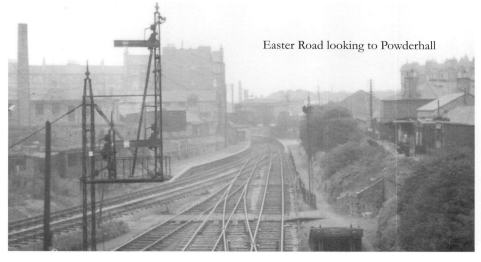

Easter Road looking to Powderhall

not the only hazard since the railway workers were often forced to cross the ECML which passed through the site and there were some fatalities.

St Margarets Engine Shed had developed to service NER locomotives for the runs between Edinburgh and Newcastle but the NBR soon reached an agreement to share the accommodation and even built some locomotives at St Margarets before switching to Cowlairs in Glasgow. The locomotive shed, listed in British Railway days as engine shed 64A, was closed in 1968. Nowadays the site, originally named after an ancient medicinal well, is occupied by office blocks.

Between Waverley Station and where Piershill Junction was later built, two short-lived stations were located. West of St Margarets shed on the ECML was Meadowbank Station unofficially known as Queens or Queens Park and sometimes used by royalty en route to Holyrood Palace. Opened in 1850 and closed by 1906, the station replaced Jock's Lodge, a short-lived station, which opened in 1848 and closed in July of the same year. It was further east, closer to where Piershill Junction was later built. North of this station but on the Piershill to Powderhall route, another Meadowbank station was opened to serve Meadowbank stadium when the Commonwealth Games were held there for a second time in 1986. Although it was only in use for two years, its platforms remain in a cutting next to the stadium. Also in the area near Piershill Junction but located on the line to Powderhall, was Piershill Station, opened in 1868, and finally closed in 1964.

At the turn of the twentieth century, rumours emerged that a new Caledonian branch (the Leith New Lines) was to be built to serve the people of Leith prompting further line construction by the NBR. With the supposed advantage of having a centrally and more conveniently sited station in Leith, a mile long double tracked branch was built to a new station at the other end of Leith Walk from the existing NBR station. From London Road Junction, east of Abbeyhill Station, the branch

89

crossed over the route from Piershill Junction and passed the home of Hibernian Football Club before reaching a grand station called Leith Central, opened in 1903, at the junction of Leith Walk and Duke Street. Some local residents were displaced as tenements were demolished to make way for the railway which entered the new station by a bridge over Easter Road. For seventeen years from 1950, a halt was provided for football fans in the cutting next to Easter Road stadium. A further short spur was provided from the Piershill line to the Leith Central line near Easter Road (Lochend South Junction).

The 'Sub'

Another route, opened in 1884 and operated from the beginning by the NBR was the Edinburgh, Suburban and Southside Junction Railway. It formed a circular route from Haymarket Junction to Gorgie Junction and then east to the old Edinburgh and Dalkeith line at Duddingston and from there to Portobello and back through Waverley to Haymarket via the Abbeyhill and Piershill loop (Inner Circle). With the re-modelling and expansion of Waverley Station in the 1890s, an island platform was built for the use of the suburban circle. The circle was broken with the opening of Leith Central in October 1903 which became the eastern terminus for the route. At over nine miles in length, this route again lost out in terms of directness to the trams but was useful for allowing freight trains to avoid passing through Waverley. The passenger service was withdrawn in September 1962 but it was kept open for freight.

Corstorphine

The final NBR route north of the main line was a branch to Corstorphine which already had a station named after it on the intercity line but this was three quarters of a mile south of what was then a small village. With the CR investigating the possibility of opening a suburban circle from Barnton south through Corstorphine to Dalry Road, the NBR decided to build the mile and a quarter branch west of Haymarket Station. Stations were initially provided at Pinkhill and Corstorphine and in 1934 Balgreen Halt was opened where the branch left the main line on the site of a previous temporary station.

Caledonian Railway Branches

The CR rated the ports of Granton and Leith as a potentially rich source of revenue but difficult landowners and the EGR's refusal to allow a connection at its Haymarket Station, and then by North Bridge Station and Scotland Street tunnel to Granton and Leith, prevented their early plans from coming to fruition. Eventually a one and a quarter mile section was built from Slateford Junction on the Caledonian's Midcalder route to Haymarket but ended disappointingly for the company in a bay platform at Haymarket Station with no direct connection to the Waverley Station route; so near and yet so far.

Progress was finally achieved when The Duke of Buccleuch, who wanted some competition for the NBR, helped to promote, with the CR, a branch from Granton Junction, between Slateford and Haymarket Station, north to Granton Harbour. From the harbour, sub-branches were constructed to the Western Breakwater and one to the eastern pier which connected with the ELGR line. The line opened in 1861 and the CR bought out the Duke's share two years later. Now that the CR had moved into the area, they immediately began to plan the next step: a goods line to Leith to provide a more convenient route for businesses west of Edinburgh. A two and three quarter mile extension from Crewe Junction, about a mile south of Granton Harbour, through Pilton and Newhaven to Leith Docks was the result and it began operation in 1864.

The Caley and the NBR routes were now starting to criss-cross each other as the railway network in the area developed. A spur was built from Pilton Junction West to Pilton Junction East to allow through running between Granton and Leith harbours and a further spur from Dalry Junction on the Lothian Road to Coltbridge route on the Granton branch, provided yet another through route.

By 1878, the Caley had wrested a large section of the increasing freight traffic to the docks from the NBR. However, the Granton line did not carry passengers until that year, when a short section of track was laid, parallel to but south of the goods line, from Craighall Road, west of Newhaven Station, to a new station, known as Leith North, next to Lindsay Road at the Port of Leith. Intermediate stations were built at Murrayfield, Craigleith, Granton Road and Newhaven and further stations were opened at Dalry Road (1900) and later still in LMSR days at East Pilton (1934)

A short branch was opened in 1894 from north of Craigleith Station to Barnton (originally named Cramond Brig) with an intermediate station at Davidson's Mains (originally named Barnton Gate). In 1937, a halt at House O'Hill was opened to try to develop local business but a plan to continue the branch south through North Gyle and Corstorphine to create a suburban loop never progressed.

Grand plans were always in the company's thinking. Having co-operated with the NBR to create Edinburgh Dock at Leith, the company produced plans in 1889 to provide an extension from near Newhaven Station south-east under Ferry Road, over the Water of Leith and Leith Walk before looping round towards Edinburgh Dock at Seafield. Known as the Leith New Lines, it was intended to open another station at Newhaven, south of the existing Newhaven Station along with new stations at Ferry Road, Leith Walk and Lochend before reaching a goods terminus, Leith East, in the dockland area almost on the opposite side of the street from the NBR station at South Leith. There was also an extension over Seafield Road into the docks. This scheme added to the density of lines and stations in the area and,

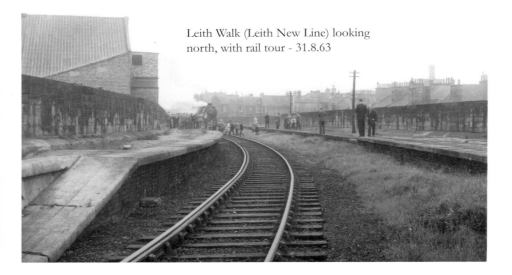

Leith Walk (Leith New Line) looking north, with rail tour - 31.8.63

arriving late on in the railway building era, meant that all the easy and less expensive options had already been taken. It took ten years for the work to start and around four years to build. The CR must have wished that they hadn't bothered. The stations never opened and the route survived on goods traffic and the odd special for railway enthusiasts.

Another proposed extension of the Leith New Lines was even more ambitious but was never built. From near Easter Road Stadium, initially by embankments and viaducts and then a tunnel under Calton Hill to St James Square and along George Street, the line was to be extended to a junction with the main line at Princes Street. Whereas the Leith folk saw advantages, the Edinburgh folk saw chaos since streets would have to be dug up. The NBR were alarmed until they realised that the plans would involve breaching the Scotland Street tunnel. The tunnel was only being used for growing mushrooms at the time but the NBR convinced the planners that it was a critical railway link by showing them that the lines were still in situ and the proposal was killed off.

The CR's original Edinburgh terminus was at Lothian Road where facilities were modest mainly due to financial problems which led to the original plans being down-graded. However, to cope with increased traffic, Princes Street Station, built slightly to the north with the ends of the platforms extending over Haymarket tunnel, was opened in May 1870 and Lothian Road was then only used for goods traffic. The station burnt down in 1890 and the company replaced it with an even grander station with classical Greek overtones and a magnificent steel framed glass roof, 850 feet long and 1000 feet wide (at its widest point). Six years later, the frontage towards Princes Street gained an extra four storeys to provide an hotel (The Caledonian Hotel) to rival the North British Hotel at the other end of Princes Street; such was the competitive vanity of Scotland's premier railway companies.

On the approach to Princes Street Station at Dalry Junction, where the Leith and Glasgow lines parted, sat Dalry Road Station (opened in 1900 and closed in 1962) and the Caledonian's Dalry Road engine shed. This shed never attained the status of Haymarket or St Margarets and after the re-organisation of 1923 seemed relegated in importance. The railway track between Dalry Road and Princes Street has now become the Western Approach Road and nothing remains of the engine shed which closed in 1965. So, sadly, much of the central hub of the CR's operation in Edinburgh centred around Princes Street Station, Dalry Road Shed and the Granton branch south of the inter city route has been demolished. The final indignity for the company's supporters came when the intercity line from Glasgow was diverted to Haymarket, partly using an upgraded industrial siding. Too late, long after the demise of the Caledonian Railway Company, their intercity route gained access to Waverley Station. The company's fierce battle for a foothold in Edinburgh was ultimately unsuccessful and only the intercity route remains open.

Exploring the Railway Heritage

All the routes in this chapter are covered by the following maps: Landranger 66; Explorer 350.

Canal Street to Granton Harbour and the branch to Leith Citadel – North British Railways

Access to the walk: the northern portal of the Scotland Street tunnel can be found in the King George V Park off Eyre Place. Going east along Eyre Place

Leith Citadel branch near Bonnington Station. Railway bridge in background carried the Leith New Line route

to Broughton Road, the trackbed of the former railway can be accessed next to the Tesco Superstore where it forms part of the Water of Leith Cycle Path. All the NBR routes can be traced and form parts of official cycle paths. There were stations at Scotland Street (0.6 mile from Waverley Station), and Trinity (2 miles). On the Leith Citadel route, there were stations at Bonnington (1.5 miles from Waverley Station), Junction Bridge (almost 2 miles) and Leith Citadel (2 miles). Junction Road Station, beneath North Junction Street was known as Junction Bridge from 1923. Only 330 yards and a tunnel separated the last two stations on this branch.

Remarkably, this route has survived. The tunnel under the New Town remains intact but with no access and since its closure over 135 years ago, it has found many uses. At least one set of rails and the rollers for the tow rope were in position until the start of the Second World War. Before 1887, it was used to store wagons but then its damp interior played host to a mushroom farm, which thrived for 42

94

years, until a parasite caused production to cease. During the Second World, the tunnel, seventy feet underground, was ideal as a bombproof underground control centre for the LNER capable of protecting up to three thousand people. Later, it was used as a laboratory by the Physics Department of Edinburgh University for research into sub-atomic particles. More recently, after the Second World War, the northern end, despite the gradient, was used by Cochrane's Garage as a store for new cars, presumably with handbrakes on! Recent talk even considered the tunnel for development as a shopping mall or part of a metro system. The Canal Street end survived for many years until the rebuilding of Waverley Station in 1897 removed any trace of Canal Street Station and closed up the tunnel. When Princes Mall was opened on the site of the Waverley Market, this underground relic of the railway era was opened up. The entrance, visible behind a grille, is found on the northern extremity of Waverley Station beside platform 19. The sign above it reads 'Site of the original Edinburgh-Leith-Newhaven Railway'. From here, it was downhill to Scotland Street 1,052 yards away. Thieves used the tunnel in 1979 as an escape route after stealing mailbags from Waverley Station. The bags were discovered near the Scotland Street portal.

Today, the journey from Waverley Station to Scotland Street has to be made above ground across Princes Street, north along St Andrews Street and Dublin

Scotland Street looking to northern portal of tunnel

Street and around Drummond Place leading to Scotland Street. The owners of the towering houses and businesses of the New Town are probably unaware of the tunnel underneath. Drummond Place overlooks Scotland Street Adventure Centre for children, part of King George V Park, which was the site of Scotland Street Station, originally known as Canonmills Station. It's a gloomy site restricted by high retaining walls on two sides, one of which contained the original entrance to the Scotland Street tunnel (254751). The dimensions of the tunnel at 24 feet wide and 17 feet high are apparent from this end although it is only possible to look a short distance into the tunnel as a brick wall, a few feet behind the metal fence, blocks the view.

A short distance across the park is the entrance to the 148 yard Rodney Street tunnel. The gap between the tunnels was deliberate so that passengers could board or leave the trains outwith the confines of the tunnels. The sudden appearance of the trains out of the Scotland Street tunnel, with guards applying the brakes, impressed no less than Robert Louis Stevenson who wrote about it. A metal fence bars exploration of the Rodney Street tunnel but at least a clear view of the tunnel's interior is possible since it remains in good condition at this end and trailing plants soften the entrance. For most of its working life, this provided the entrance into Scotland Street Goods Depot which was sited here after the closure of the Scotland Street tunnel. Sidings fanned out to the west in what was a tight space to work. Given that there was no railway access to the south after the closure of the Scotland Street tunnel, it is surprising that the depot remained open until 1968 when the last of the daily fish trains from Leith Citadel to the goods depot ended. A year earlier, it had stopped handling domestic coal deliveries.

A detour through the King George V Park on to Eyre Place and east to Broughton Road leads to the northern portal (Heriothill end) of the Rodney Street tunnel beside the Tesco Store on Broughton Road but the tunnel entrance is blocked by piles of earth. The tunnel will soon be re-opened for use by cyclists. There was once an engine shed at Heriothill (254752) where the store now stands.

The trackbed has been converted into the Water of Leith cycle path and continues north over the Water of Leith by a skewed three span bridge which has curved wing-walls of ashlar masonry and pilasters separating the spans. The bridge, known as the Warriston Rail Bridge (253754), crosses both Warriston Road and the Water of Leith and is a listed structure (category B). Over the bridge stood a small signal box controlling Warriston Junction where the line to North Leith Station branched north-east. Preserved as a walkway, the original Newhaven railway line continues north between Warriston Cemetery on the right and then Goldenacre Sports Ground on the left mostly in a tree-lined cutting as the trackbed cut through the higher ground to the north of the river. The route passes under two overbridges, one of which carries Ferry Road (listed category B) before reaching Trinity Junction (250763) where the former line from Piershill Junction joins it. There is a distinctly rural feel to the scene in spite of it being in the centre of a large city.

Another cycle track crosses at the site of Trinity Junction which now serves as a junction for five cycle routes. In the past, the CR to Leith crossed over the

Trinity line just north of Trinity Junction by a bridge which has now been removed. Beyond the line of the Caley railway, the Trinity branch enters the 144 yard Trinity tunnel (listed category C). It forms part of a pleasant walkway where trains once headed down towards the Forth. The final overbridge at Lennox Row is also listed (Category C), the last of a line of listed remnants for this historic route. High buttressed retaining walls line the cutting before the track veers westwards to the

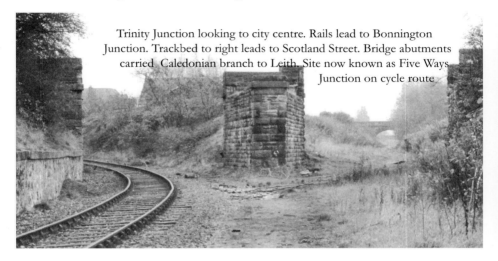

Trinity Junction looking to city centre. Rails lead to Bonnington Junction. Trackbed to right leads to Scotland Street. Bridge abutments carried Caledonian branch to Leith. Site now known as Five Ways Junction on cycle route

site of the second Trinity Station (249769). The original goods yard site, now occupied by flats, is glimpsed between the retaining wall and the former station. The original station, known as Trinity and Newhaven, was to the right of the second station at the edge of the former goods yard which closed in 1925. Of the second station, the curved platforms are still intact and while the passengers on the train saw a single-storey building with twin gables each of which had a bay window, the passengers walking up from Trinity Crescent to the rear saw the full extent of the building which was in fact two storeys high at the back. The station once had two booking office windows: one to serve the general public and the other for the use of the fisherwomen who carted fish to the city. This prevented other travellers' hands from becoming oily and smelly since the fisherwomens' hands were usually covered in fish scales.

Beyond the Trinity Station, the line curved as it crossed over Granton Road. It was a quick climb (at a gradient of 1 in a 100) from the shoreline round a tight curve for trains heading towards Edinburgh. The eastern abutment of the railway bridge over Granton Road remains. The track then continued along the shoreline towards the middle pier of Granton Harbour where there was a simple station which on closure was used as a boatyard. This last section has been landscaped with only an overbridge surviving. Visible in the distance to the west is the Forth Railway Bridge which precipitated the demise of this route.

Trinity Crescent runs down to Chain Pier. Opened in 1821 at a cost of £4000, the pier was four feet wide and 500 feet long and consisted of a wooden walkway suspended from chains anchored in a series of pillars. Unfortunately, it was never very practical and was swept away during a storm in 1898. Pleasant afternoon cruises sailed from here to Alloa, Grangemouth and Stirling although they had to compete with those willing to 'spend a penny' to use the pier to swim round and for bathing.

Leith Citadel

The section to Leith Citadel which branched off at Warriston Junction, crossed an elaborate bridge over an access road to Warriston Cemetery and continued towards Bonnington Junction. It crossed the line from Piershill Junction to Trinity by a level crossing. South of the Leith Citadel line, a few hundred yards away in the direction of Piershill Junction, stood Powderhall Station which was next to the road bridge that carried Broughton Road over the line. This line was closed then re-opened to a new terminus just beyond Powderhall Station and is now used by Edinburgh City Council to transport refuse from the Powderhall Compaction Plant to Oxwellmains Cement Works in East Lothian. The refuse plant buildings dominate the skyline at this point. A short stretch of the former railway between Powderhall and Bonnington Junction still exists. When in operation, there was a signal box on this section and a spur was added to ease the flow of traffic between

Powderhall Station - looking towards Granton

the two routes. Bonnington South Junction ran in a curve beside the Water of Leith. The second spur to the north of the level crossing was Bonnington North Junction. Little remains of either spur with a housing estate having covered most of the northern spur. The two spurs merged with the line to Leith Citadel near to the point where the CR route to South Leith later crossed over.

The Caledonian South Leith branch crossed over the NBR route and the Water of Leith by a massive girder bridge. The northern abutments and two piers of this bridge remain. The Leith Citadel route then entered a cutting as it approached Newhaven Road where Bonnington Station (260762) was located in a gloomy site overlooked by high tenements. Long platforms, which still exist although partly used as a garden, curved under the road bridge with steep winding stone steps leading up to the road. Despite its cramped conditions, this station was the busiest on a busy route. The station house to the east of the Newhaven Road bridge over the railway, at number 94 Newhaven Road, was dwarfed in later years by four-storey tenements lining Newhaven Road. Beyond the station are the truncated remains of the West Bowling Goods depot which extended south over the Water of Leith to a private siding.

The route then passed under Fort Street before running alongside the river to another station called Junction Road at North Junction Street. The freight depot at Junction Bridge, as Junction Road was then called, closed in 1961. From here a 137 yard tunnel led to the cramped site at North Leith, later to be known as Leith Citadel (266767) to avoid confusion with Caledonian station. The station at Junction Road and the tunnel have gone but the Leith Citadel station buildings remain opposite the warehouses on Commercial Street and now house the Citadel Youth Centre. The main entrance is flanked by ornate pillars extending above the roofline which give the station a classical look. The engine shed has been replaced by houses and the warehouses, like many such buildings in Leith, have been converted into flats.

Back at Bonnington Junction and north of the level crossing site, the Piershill Junction branch winds north-west towards Granton becoming another pleasant tree-lined cutting. The piers of an old overbridge remain south of Ferry Road which the railway passed under before reaching Trinity Junction and linking up with the original route to Granton.

Leith Central Line

Very little remains of this one and a quarter mile branch. The site of Leith Central is the most interesting relic and something of the sheer scale of the station can still be recognised today. Trains left the main line at Abbeyhill Junction (270742) and swept into Abbeyhill Station over a railway bridge after a hundred yards. The

Leith Central signalbox - 20.1.87

station was located west of London Road with booking offices sited at street level. Covered stairways led down to the platforms with the brick buildings on each side of the railway track having a canopy extending the width of the platform. One platform and the rails survive, now hemmed in by a block of new flats. Looking west from London Road, Arthur's Seat provides a prominent backdrop. The station was extremely busy with one hundred trains a day at the beginning of the First World War, although by the end of the Second World War this had reduced by more than half. Today, the station site is undergoing redevelopment.

On the east side of London Road was London Road Junction where the branch to Leith Central began its mile-long journey. To the left was a spur to the Piershill Junction to Trinity line and just before the railway bridge over the Piershill line which carried the Leith Central branch, there was another spur to the Piershill line at Lochend South Junction. In a triangular area of only several hundred yards there was a multitude of branches. Only the Piershill line leading to Powderhall remains but it is now single track. The area is an unattractive wasteland but problems of access probably prevent this confined space from being redeveloped. After leaving Lochend North Junction where another spur from the Piershill line joined, the route to Leith Central passed to the south of Easter Road stadium through a deep cutting which has been filled in and a tarmac path crosses the area. Easter Road Halt, no trace of which remains, consisted of a single platform with a steep railed path connecting it to the football stadium. Blocks of flats have been built near the stadium.

The route then passed under a three-arched brick bridge at Hawkhill Avenue which has been partly filled in. The line disappears at the edge of the Leith Academy playing fields where it crosses a cycle path which once formed part of the CR's Leith South branch. All traces of the bridge which once carried that line over the NBR line have gone. The NBR branch continued to the rear of the houses on Lochend Road before turning towards Leith Walk and reaching Leith Central Station by a plate girder bridge over Easter Road. A section of tenements on Easter Road was demolished to make way for the railway and tenements have now been rebuilt to fill the gap left by its removal!

Leith Central Station consisted of a huge glass cavern over sixty feet high, supported by girder work, which broadened from 100 feet at the Easter Road end to more than double that width. Four tracks led into this cathedral of the railway era with sure foundations built on sturdy masonry walls. At the Leith Walk end, the station buildings dominated both Leith Walk and the corner of Duke Street. The railway clock was so prominent that the local council paid for its maintenance and the electricity to keep it going. The size of the structure amazed locals and even after a serious fire in 1937 which destroyed one of the island platforms, business continued as usual. It was bad news however, for the many pigeons nesting in the glass canopy which were overcome by the smoke. Dead pigeons on the track; in those days the trains continued to run!

Today, the site (270758) is occupied by a supermarket and Leith Waterworld but this icon of a bygone age, when railway rivalries overtook financial sense, is still an impressive site. It has been excavated and the original station level is now fifteen feet above the car park of the supermarket. It was used as a maintenance depot for diesel multiple units after it closed for passengers in 1952. The electrification of the Edinburgh trams in the 1920s which allowed through journeys to Princes Street, made the train less convenient and revenues tailed off. This was a great pity for what was an impressive suburban station. The station buildings facing Leith Walk and Duke Street still remain along with the imposing clock. Sadly, little remains of this branch and in the near future probably even more will disappear.

North British Corstorphine Branch

Access to the walk: the trackbed has been preserved and can be accessed from the railway bridge over Balgreen Road. The branch left the main line at Haymarket West Junction and had stations at Balgreen Halt (0.25 mile from the junction), Pinkhill (0.75 mile) and Corstorphine (1.5 miles)

Corstorphine had a station on the Edinburgh and Glasgow line from 1842, the only problem being that it lay three quarters of a mile south of what was then a small village in the shadow of Corstorphine Hill. This early station could not compete with the horse- drawn route east through Murrayfield to the city. It needed a threat from the Caley to build a line south from Barnton and east to Dalry Station before a railway was brought closer to the village and in 1902, Corstorphine gained a station that was truly local and the original Corstorphine Station became Saughton Station.

What was proposed, was a mile and a half double track branch, the first quarter mile of which ran parallel to the main line before veering north-west after crossing Balgreen Road. The route then passed to the east and wound around the north of Carrick Knowe Golf Course before reaching the site of Pinkhill Station and shortly afterwards, Corstorphine Station. The route is now a cycle path but since the terminus site occupied a large tract of land, it became a magnet for property developers and has been redeveloped.

The start (219724) is easily found beside the railway overbridge on Balgreen Road. A path leads up to the four-track main line which stretches east towards Haymarket Station and the Castle and west towards the Forth Railway Bridge and Glasgow. The branch veered away from the main line, a short distance east, where the main line crossed the Water of Leith. The site of Balgreen Halt, opened in 1934 as a late addition to the route, is beside Balgreen Road. Jenners Furniture Depositry lies to the north and overshadows the site. The station, of which nothing remains, was simple with curved platforms and basic buildings but was handily situated for potential passengers when Saughtonhall, the area to the north of the main line, was developed. A temporary station had already occupied the site in 1908 when the Scottish National Exhibition was held at Saughton Park. The route passes between the golf course and the western edge of Saughtonhall with views contrasting between the golfers and the end of numerous cul de sacs. Now on an embankment, it crosses over the access road to the golf course by a simple plate-girder bridge and a low two-arch skewed bridge before swinging west towards the site of Pinkhill Station.

Pinkhill Station site (211728) is largely intact. Only the station buildings on

Pinkhill Station buildings today

the curved platforms have been removed including the wooden ticket office. The main station buildings were located on the steep gradient of Pinkhill Road which crossed the line before turning sharply right. They were built beside the road but slightly separate and steps led down to the platforms. A sign on the platform stated 'ALIGHT HERE FOR THE ZOOLOGICAL PARK'. Edinburgh Zoo is a short distance across the nearby busy Corstorphine Road. The underside of the road bridge over the railway has now gained extra support to stop subsidence. The stretch around Pinkhill Station has the only section of cutting on the branch. Engineering the line was certainly not difficult with the height fairly constant at 150 feet. Office blocks hem in the short stretch of trackbed leading to Corstorphine Station site (202728) now occupied by a housing estate known as Paddockholm which ends on Station Road. The single-storey station building, which was at the end of the long platforms, has been demolished and the only reminder of the station is a stone boundary wall to the north. A century ago, 24 trains a day ran on the branch line but when it closed at the end of December 1967 only the penguins in the nearby zoo would have missed it.

Caledonian Routes

The section between Princes Street Station and Dalry Junction is now the Western Approach Road. The line between Dalry Junction and Slateford Junction was part of the Caledonian line from Midcalder Junction to Princes Street and still exists as a walkway and then as an access road (from Harrison Place) to Slateford Civil Engineer Depot. Near the start of the access road was Merchiston Station (233720) where only the foundations of the platforms remain.

The section between Dalry Junction and Coltbridge Junction, the start of the Leith branch, is now isolated from the rest of the route to Leith North by the removal of the former CR bridge over the Glasgow to Edinburgh main line. There are few surviving remnants between the two junctions. However, what lies to the north of the inter-city route has been largely preserved as a cycle path albeit with a few changes, none of which stop a pleasant exploration of a branch that swung north then sharply east to reach Leith with branches west to Barnton then north to Granton Harbour and finally from Newhaven Junction to South Leith.

Access to the walk: there are many access points to the branches but to explore the entire length, the trackbed is best picked up north of the main line south of Roseburnter West, on the A8 at Balbirnie Place, next to flats, a short distance from Haymarket Station. There were stations at Murrayfield (next to Balbirnie Place), Craigleith (0.75 miles), East Pilton (2 miles), Granton Road 2.5 miles), Newhaven (3.5 miles), Leith North (4 miles).

The start of the route from Balbirnie Place (234729) is on an embankment allowing good views to the west over the Haymarket Sprinter Depot, Tynecastle (home of Heart of Midlothian Football Club) and Murrayfield (home of the Scottish Rugby Union). Much drama and often shattered dreams are wrapped up in the last two places along with the rare moment of glory. At least, the railway depot is more reliable and less prone to crises. The familiar city centre sites are visible to the east along with views of the George Donaldson School for the Deaf with its distinctive green-roofed turrets. The route passed over Roseburnter West by a railway bridge with an interesting recess for workmen still bearing the stencil EPTD and an elaborate motif in the side metalwork of the bridge depicting two lions on the outside with three flowers: a thistle, a rose and a shamrock in the middle.

Trees grow in profusion along each side of the track transforming the nature of the route. Murrayfield Station opened in 1878, seventeen years after the line began as a freight line. Sited at Roseburn Terrace, it provided easy access to Murrayfield for rugby specials on match day. Some of the long platforms remain and look as if they were extended in length to accommodate the specials. Shrouded by trees, the present-day scene seems peaceful which must be a contrast to the emotions on display on long ago match days.

Built on high ground, the railway avoided the local flooding problems caused by the Water of Leith which it crossed (shortly after the station) by the high three-arch stone bridge (231735) known as the Murrayfield Viaduct. Deep cuttings took the railway through some of the outer edges of Corstorphine Hill and it was crossed by road bridges at Ralveston Dykes and Queensferry Road.

Next to Queensferry Road another station, Craigleith (223747), was located a short distance to the east of the large Craigleith Quarry which provided the creamy sandstone to build many of Edinburgh's buildings. The quarry is now a retail park.

Leith to Edinburgh train at Craigleith Station 11.1.58

Passengers had a steep climb to road level as evidenced by the station platforms which are still in situ at the bottom of a cutting.

Slightly north, the branch to Barnton which did not open until 1894 forked at Craigleith Junction. The Craigleith Junction site has a route marker erected by Sustrans and it's possible to reach the Forth Bridge from here but this requires a deviation from the original railway route. After Craigleith Junction, the route veers north-east and passes under Telford Road. The first break in the line is at Ferry Road where a new metal girder bridge has been erected to carry cyclists over the road. Near this point was Crewe Junction where the Granton Branch left. This branch has suffered more than the others. The West Granton Access Road has been built over it as far as Granton Road and while a short section exists north of

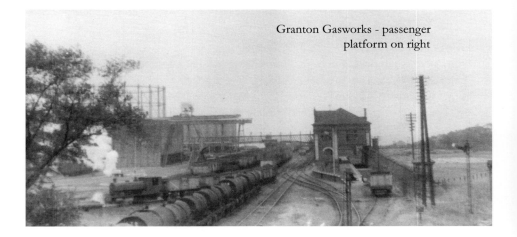

Granton Gasworks - passenger platform on right

this, where the line curved towards the harbour, the rest of the route is part of a development site for Waterfront Edinburgh and is unlikely to survive.

The gasworks at Granton had a short branch and a private station for the workers which until 1942 had its own service to Princes Street. The workers were offered only third class fares on this restricted service and there was never a public passenger service. While not as attractive as the Castle, the towering gasworks, once the largest in Scotland, were just as prominent a landmark for those in the north of the city before they were demolished.

The route to Leith now turned east passing behind Telford College and crossing over Crewe Road North before reaching the eastern end of a triangular junction at Pilton Junction North which eased access to Granton Harbour. Behind Morrisons Superstore and next to Pilton Drive beside the overbridge was East Pilton Halt (234760). A simply constructed station consisting only of platforms and wooden

East Pilton looking to Leith - 11.1.58

buildings, it was opened in 1934 to serve the engineering works of Parsons Peebles, now relocated to Leith after a fire. A leisure centre and a new housing estate now occupy the site but some evidence of the platforms appears to exist in the undergrowth. The film 'Trainspotting', based on Irvine Welsh's book about the life of young drug addicts in Edinburgh, was set in the estates in the Pilton area.

This section of the route had many overbridges often added in later years to provide access for new developments. The station at Granton Road has also gone and it, like the next station at Newhaven, was an 'add on'. Built later and separately supported by girders, there was a small gap between the road bridge and the single-storey buildings at Granton Road station which were built at road level with steps leading down to the platforms. No trace of the station remains.

The route continues through a wide, deep cutting and once crossed over the NBR line to Trinity but this bridge has been demolished and the trackbed now crosses the line on the level. The line carries on to Newhaven Junction (253765)

Granton Road Station looking towards Leith - 20.2.55

which was the junction for the 'goods only' branch to South Leith. The site is now a wildflower meadow. Craighall Sidings were sited here and there is some evidence of the loading banks amongst the trees. From here, the original freight line ran parallel to the later passenger line with the result that four tracks passed under Newhaven Road. Newhaven Station, on Craighall Road, which is overlooked by Trinity Academy has survived, part of the site being used by a garage. The station building was used as a joiner's workshop for many years until the business closed. Tenements straddle the trackside as the route widens, shortly before passing under Lindsay Road to reach the terminus at Leith North. The station started simply as Leith, was renamed North Leith in 1903 and then in 1952, in British Railways days, it was changed to Leith North. The NBR's former station in Leith was originally

Leith North Station - 7.6.58

called Leith North but was better known in latter days as Leith Citadel. These name changes must have been confusing for those using the railways.

Road re-alignment has changed the layout near the Leith North terminus but the Caley Bar on the corner of Portland Street gives a clue as to where it was. The station, which has recently been demolished, consisted of an island platform partly covered by a simple shed and there were no facilities to allow the locomotive to change ends for the return journey. The solution to this problem was to push the carriages up the gradient out of the station then allow the engine to uncouple and go into a siding where it waited until the carriages ran back down the slope to the station. Diesel multiple units worked the line for the last three years before its closure in 1962.

Given that the whole area around the station is undergoing an amazing transformation with both the Scottish Executive buildings and the Royal Yacht Britannia at Ocean Terminal within a quarter of a mile, then the prospects for the line if it had remained open would have been very different. A similar argument could be made for Leith Citadel just half a mile along the road and it's sad that neither route survived.

The Craigleith to Barnton Branch

This short branch, double track and only two and three quarter miles in length, opened for both passenger and goods traffic in 1894. It started at Craigleith Junction

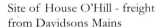

Site of House O'Hill - freight
from Davidsons Mains

just north of Craigleith Station and climbed fifty feet to the summit at Davidson's Mains before dropping fifty feet to the terminus at Barnton. A halt at House O'Hill between the junction and Davidson's Mains was a later addition in 1937.

Access to the walk: the trackbed can be accessed from the walkway linking Balbirnie Place to Leith or from South Groathill Avenue next to Craigleith Retail Park. The former branch line has become a cycle path as far as Davidson's Mains. Thereafter the cycle route to South Queensferry deviates from the line of the former railway.

The route was the first section of the CR's vision of a circle from Barnton south through North Gyle and Corstorphine and back to Princes Street but this never

108

materialised, with the competing NBR branch to Corstorphine certainly a factor. The branch settled down to meet the needs of this expanding residential area of north-west Edinburgh with the provision of a frequent and fast service. To begin with, 24 trains a day made the sixteen minute journey to Princes Street Station but by the 1930s this was down to 20. The opening of the halt at House O'Hill was an attempt by the railway to generate further business but the rise in car ownership provided stiff competition and the route closed to passengers in 1951. The section to Davidson's Mains was left open for goods traffic but even this stump finally closed in 1960.

At the site of Craigleith Junction, a Sustrans route marker shows the different paths it is possible to take. The route towards South Queensferry starts on an embankment which quickly changes into a cutting as it passes under the brick-lined overbridge carrying Telford Road. Due to the rising gradient, there are superb views back towards the centre of the city. On the left, where Corbiehill Avenue and House O'Hill Avenue meet, was House O'Hill Halt (215753). It was next to a skewed-arch sandstone bridge which carries Main Street over the former railway. In the grass verge, the possible foundations of the platform remain.

After a further overbridge, the former trackbed is found on a tree-covered embankment, to the right of the path, which ends suddenly at South Cramond Road. No trace remains of Davidson's Mains Station (204756). To the left, a supermarket occupies the site of the goods yard. Situated on the west side of the road, the main passenger station buildings with their brick chimneys were fairly modest and a metal lattice footbridge provided a link to the opposite platform where there was a small waiting room. Houses now occupy the site. From here, new housing covers the route, apart from a short section occupied by sports grounds. The route snaked to the south of the Royal Burgess Golf Course before reaching Barnton

Barnton Station - 2.10.46

Remnant of Barnton line - overbridge near Barnton Station used as garage

Station (186750) behind the Barnton Hotel. The station had an unroofed island platform with the buildings to the rear. The station building site is now occupied by a newsagent but behind flats at Barnton Grove close to the former station, an overbridge has survived with the archway being used as a garage.

Newhaven Junction to South Leith – 'Leith New Lines'

Some sections of this branch remain and it is worth exploring even if it requires several detours. The branch is best explored from Newhaven Junction. The effort that went into the construction of this route was remarkable. It was the CR's final incursion into the Leith area. A grand master plan was behind it, as described earlier, to provide a route from Leith under Princes Street back to Princes Street Station and give further access to the Edinburgh Docks on the Leith waterfront.

From Newhaven Junction (253765) west of Newhaven Station on the Leith North line, the route headed south-west until it reached Craighall Road where a second Newhaven Station was opened to give two Caledonian stations within a hundred yards! The platforms were built, as they were for the rest of the stations on the route, but no further building was completed nor were any of the stations opened. Nothing of this second station can be found in what is now Victoria Park. A proposed spur to form a triangular junction with the Leith North line at Newhaven Road was prepared but the rails were never laid. At the southern end of Victoria Park is Ferry Road where a station was planned and platforms built. New buildings have removed any trace of this unopened station. Chancelot

Granton branch to left with Leith Citadel branch from Bonnington South junction. Original Chancelot Mills in centre

Mills sidings were also located here. The imposing mill buildings were demolished in 1972 and the business relocated to Leith Docks. The trackbed, now a cycle path, passed between two rows of tenements before rising to cross over the NBR line to the west of Bonnington Station and the Water of Leith. The sandstone abutments to the north have been turned into a sitting area named Steadfast Gate, to commemorate a local connection with the Boys Brigade. Two round sandstone piers, which helped to support the plate girder bridge, remain. New housing and an industrial estate have obliterated the next section to the south of the river.

Taking the Water of Leith cycle path which follows the old NBR route, Bonnington Station is reached and climbing to street level at Newhaven Road, it can be followed south to its junction with Bonnington Road at Bonnington

Abutments of Water of Leith railbridge (Leith New Line). NBR trackbed to left of bench. Near Bonnington Station (see page 94)

Toll. The abutments of the former girder bridge which crossed Bonnington Toll diagonally can be seen next to the Scotsman buildings. Rosebank or Bonnington Goods Yard was located here. Across the bridge, the railway ran parallel to Bonnington Road before veering south-east across Pilrig Park to Leith Walk where another goods station, Leith Walk West Goods, was located. From here, the railway arches and bridge over Leith Walk started. From Jane Street, next to the arches (now mainly occupied by the motor trade), the abutments on both sides of Leith Walk can be seen. Crossing Leith Walk and going down Manderston Street, more railway arches are found which now end at Halmyre Street. A short distance away, on the other side of Easter Road, once crossed by yet another girder bridge, is Thorntreeside where a cycle path follows the trackbed of the former Caley line

Abutments of Leith New Line
over Leith Walk

around the playing fields of Leith Academy. A few hundred yards to the north the NBR's Leith Central Station was situated. At the southern end of what are now the school's playing fields, the Caley branch crossed over the NBR branch to Leith Central station near Hawkhill Avenue. The bridge has been removed.

The branch then passed under Lochend Road and continued in a wide cutting towards the docks at Seafield Road. The area occupied by Restalrig Goods has not been built upon. From this point, the trackbed climbed to reach Seafield Junction before it crossed Seafield Road to get to the docks. Another section continued north towards Leith Links, parallel to Seafield Road without crossing it, on a high embankment with sandstone facing. Construction costs must have been considerable. This section now stops at Seafield Place but the original track continued as far as Salamander Place where Leith East Goods Depot was located.

This route is challenging to follow but clues remain as to the path the branch took. There is no doubt about the substantial investment made by the CR but it was a line built too late to have any hope of fulfilling its potential.

Postscript

While the original impetus to construct lines was provided by the need to reach the coast and develop the ferry trade, the development of the docks in the era after the opening of the Forth Railway Bridge in 1890, made the area still attractive to the railway companies and their intense rivalry created a dense network of branches. Buses and trams provided the real competition and the branch lines finally lost out to them. Thankfully Edinburgh Council has had the foresight to preserve most of the lines as cycle paths and these not only provide a link with the city's industrial past, but give an incentive to its inhabitants to keep fit. The routes provide a different way of getting around the city and a rewarding experience for those with an interest in industrial heritage.

Replacement of bridge on Abbeyhill Loop
(1950s) looking west towards Waverley Station

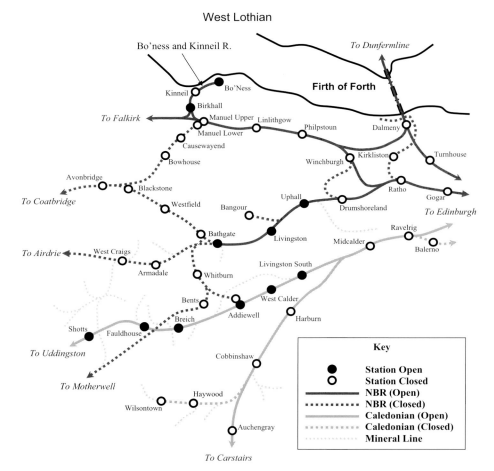

Chapter 5

Shale Oil, Coal and Corridor Traffic : West Lothian

West Lothian is the second smallest of Scotland's counties. Located to the south of the River Forth, it covers the land bounded by Edinburgh to the east, the Pentland Hills to the south-east, the hills around Leven Seat to the south and the River Avon to the west. Viewed from the Gladsmuir Hills to the south, West Lothian can be seen as the eastern end of the 'corridor county', the low lying narrow central belt linking Glasgow to Edinburgh which is criss-crossed by canals and railways. Although travellers along the M8 motorway between Scotland's two largest cities see a land scarred by the remnants of quarrying and the coal and oil shale industries, they also encounter signs of modern industry as the region seeks a new identity. The distinctive pink-coloured shale bings scattered around the countryside are a unique feature of the landscape, a very visual reminder of the oil-shale industry. Hundreds of millions of years ago when West Lothian was a tidal lagoon covered by swamps and forests, the tides deposited fine silted mud containing the remains of marine animals. The silted mud was gradually covered by limestone deposits. Compressed under these deposits, the marine remains in the silted mud were converted into oil shale deposits in a process akin to a giant pressure cooker. The dead plants and remains of the forests which didn't decay under these conditions in the usual way that woods rot, were slowly turned into coal by the same forces. Volcanoes destroyed this landscape, only for it to be slowly re-formed thus creating further deposits. This cycle of landscape creation and destruction was repeated over a long period of time trapping some of the oil shale and coal deposits deep underground.

It took the genius of John 'Paraffin' Young, in the mid nineteenth century, to tap the oil trapped in the shale and build the world's first 'oil refinery'. The chemical industry and the initiative to derive a range of products such as wax, fertilisers and caustic soda from oil were developed in West Lothian. The oil industry, with government support, survived until after the Second World War although the relatively small scale of the deposits meant that other oil-producing regions quickly overtook the Lothian oilfield. However, Scotland's contribution to the creation of the modern oil industry was significant and is sadly often forgotten.

The refining centre of the Lothian oil industry was based around Pumpherston, midway between Uphall and Midcalder and a network of mineral railways was built to compete for both the oil and coal traffic. With the closure of the oil shale industry and the coal mines, much of the evidence of these transport links has been lost whilst the raw scars these industries left are gradually being covered over by the planting of the many woodlands that will make up the Central Scotland Forest. The memories of the harsh working conditions are, however, still locked in the minds of many ex-miners and their communities. Lying to the north and south of the M8 motorway, communities such as Bathgate and Livingston new town are trying to regenerate the local economy by attracting electronic and computing companies to the area. This enterprising venture does justice to the spirit of the people who had so cleverly exploited the area's natural resources and built industries at the forefront of innovation in times past.

The railways played an important part in the development of the oil shale works, quarries and coal mines by linking them to the main lines. However, the first mode of transport to cross West Lothian was the Union Canal opened in 1822 to link the Forth and Clyde canal at Falkirk with Edinburgh. The Union Canal did not require any locks as it followed the 240 foot contour. This clever design, however, did not allow the canal to compete with the railway because the opening of the Edinburgh and Glasgow Railway (EGR) in February 1842 slashed the journey time between the two cities from eight hours by canal to two and a quarter hours by rail. The 46 mile Glasgow Queen Street to Edinburgh Haymarket route was constructed as a high speed line along the Forth and Clyde valley to the north of the Bathgate Hills with viaducts smoothing the valley crossings and tunnels and cuttings boring through rock obstacles. The major engineering works were: a long cutting to the east of Philpstoun, a 353 yard tunnel at Winchburgh and the spectacular thirty-six arch Almond Viaduct which even today draws admiring glances from motorists on the approaches to Edinburgh.

The citizens of Glasgow and Edinburgh responded enthusiastically to the new mode of transport with passenger numbers increasing to in excess of one million in just over six years. The English owned but Scottish managed EGR was a great success as the people of Central Scotland caught the travel bug; the age of the excursion was born. The railway quickly killed passenger traffic on the canals and by 1846 the EGR proposed buying them over, much to the dismay of the railway's English backers who saw no advantage in the proposals. The Scottish directors, however, were motivated by the Caledonian Railway Company's construction of lines towards Glasgow and Edinburgh which brought the 'Caley' ever closer to their territory. If this rival company took over the canal network, they could run it in direct competition to the EGR or, indeed, fill in the canals and use them as a trackbed for railways. In 1849, in response to this threat, the EGR bought over the

Union Canal as part of its preparations for the inevitable forthcoming battle with the Caledonian Railway Company (CR).

By 1848, the CR had completed routes from Carlisle to both Glasgow and Edinburgh. This gave the company a route between Scotland's two principal cities via Carstairs Junction but it was two sides of a triangle as opposed to the EGR's more direct route. This slower route along the Almond Valley, avoiding the Pentland Hills, was eight miles longer and at best took twenty-five minutes more for the journey than their rivals. Battle commenced for passengers including fare cutting which was ruinous for both companies. The EGR constructed another route between the cities although by the time it was opened, the company had been taken over by the North British Railway (NBR). This new route 'The Edinburgh and Bathgate Railway' departed from the intercity route at Bathgate Junction to the west of Ratho Station, reached Bathgate in November 1849, was extended to Coatbridge in 1862 and finally to Glasgow's College Station in 1871. It was not a fast route but it did travel through mineral rich areas and created lucrative income. A short 4 mile branch was also opened from Bathgate to link with the Monklands Railway (MR) at Blackston Junction.

Realising that they were hampered by the longer route via Carstairs, the CR constructed a more direct route through Cleland and Midcalder. Competition for the transport of passengers and minerals started again but this time between the CR and the NBR. The NBR extended south-west from Bathgate to link with an earlier railway to Morningside in Lanarkshire with their rival's lines crossing near Fauldhouse on the border between West Lothian and Lanarkshire. Further branches took the NBR to Leven Seat Quarry in West Lothian and to Shotts in Lanarkshire. Another mineral line ran from the intercity route near Winchburgh through Broxburn to Drumshoreland on the Bathgate line. The CR also opened several branches from their Edinburgh route in West Lothian from east of Breich to reach coal deposits and around Addiewell for oil shale deposits.

The NBR's successful take-over of the Edinburgh and Glasgow route in 1865 gave it the advantage in the Forth-Clyde valley and a stranglehold in Edinburgh. By purchasing the Forth and Clyde Canal Company in 1867 and its branch railway to Grangemouth, the CR succeeded in reaching the Forth. The docks at Grangemouth prospered and Bo'ness which was then part of West Lothian, a few miles to the east, suffered. The town of Bo'ness sought to restore its former position and had high hopes for an extension of the Slamannan and Borrowstounness Railway (SBR) from Causewayend (part of the Monkland Railway network), south of Bo'ness into Bo'ness Harbour. The railway, however, did not lease the harbour and traffic on the line was limited. The town appealed to the NBR who, by this time, had subsumed the MR network and a new harbour was built with borrowed money. However, the CR obtained running rights and since the NBR did not want their investment to benefit their rivals, they backed out of the project. The townsfolk of Bo'ness switched their allegiance to the CR who then obtained the rights to provide a service into Bo'ness over NBR lines but to the disappointment of the town, they did little to exploit this victory over their rivals. Ironically, some of this railway still exists due to the Scottish Railway Preservation Society which has established a successful railway attraction at Bo'ness, the Bo'ness and Kinneil Railway, so that trains still travel on some of the Bo'ness railways over fifty years after the last scheduled BR service departed.

There were many branches from the NBR intercity route (usually mineral lines) but in addition to the Bathgate route, a line was built from Winchburgh to Dalmeny in 1890 on the opening of the Forth Railway Bridge.

Today, the intercity route between Glasgow Queen Street and Edinburgh Waverley is still a vital rail link. The old Caledonian routes from Carstairs and Cleland remain along with the NBR branches to Dalmeny and Bathgate. The other lines withered and died as mineral resources were used up although there are plans to re-open the Bathgate to Airdrie route.

Railways around Bathgate

Centrally placed to take advantage of the mineral wealth of the area, Bathgate was an important railway town with an engine shed and two stations: Bathgate (Upper) to the east and Bathgate (Lower). The railway age arrived in the town in 1849 with the opening of the Edinburgh and Bathgate Railway (EBR). A 14.5 mile branch west from Bathgate to Airdrie was finished by August 1862 and, in April 1871, an alternative route between Glasgow College station and Edinburgh via Bathgate was completed.

The railway system also extended north-west from Bathgate to Blackston in 1855 and linked up with the MR which was eventually merged with the EGR on 31st July 1865. On the following day, the EGR was, in turn, absorbed by the NBR. The MR evolved out of the Monkland and Kirkintilloch Railway (MKR) which had begun operations in 1826 using horse drawn waggonways to take coal from the pits to the Forth and Clyde Canal. The network extended eastwards when the Ballochney Railway, operating in the coal mining area to the north-east of Airdrie, joined the MKR in 1828 and in 1840, the network merged with the Slamannan Railway (SR). The Slamannan Railway ran from Airdrie to Causewayend where it linked with the Union Canal. Passengers and coal travelled by a combination of railway and canal boat to reach Edinburgh. All that changed with the emergence of the EGR two years later. In 1851, the SBR opened which extended the SR from

Causewayend through Manuel (Low Level) into Bo'ness. In several places, the SR had to use stationary engines to haul coal wagons up steep inclines. There were gradients of 1 in 23 at the Airdrie end to reach Slamannan on the high plain and an equally sharp drop to Causewayend at the eastern end. The NBR ran a service from Bathgate Lower to join the SR at Blackston Junction with an intermediate station at Westfield and ran a service from the junction down to Manuel.

The Wilsontown, Morningside and Coltness Railway (WMCR) was opened in 1845 to carry coal and iron from Longridge, four miles south of Bathgate, to Chapel near Morningside in Lanarkshire. It was taken over by the EGR in 1849 and by 1852, the line along with its stations at Davies Dyke, Headless Cross and Longridge was closed. Headless Cross was situated where the trackbed crossed the B715. With competition for the coal business in the area intensifying, the NBR who had taken over the EGR in 1865 re-opened the WMCR in the same year and extended it four miles to Bathgate Upper Station to create a 14 mile branch which passed under the Caledonian line from Cleland at Fauldhouse on the county border. This re-opened line had a short branch from Whitburn to Addiewell with a number of other branches located in Lanarkshire.

The final line in the area was the short branch from the Newbridge Junction to Bathgate line which ran from Uphall to Bangour. It opened in 1905 to take staff, patients and visitors from Uphall Station to the Bangour Hospital which was used for mentally ill patients. During the First World War, the hospital was extended to become the Edinburgh War Hospital and the short branch was extensively used to bring in wounded soldiers. Many of the staff stayed at nearby Dechmont where there was a station. The branch only operated for about 15 years and, sadly, apart from bridge abutments in Dechmont village and a mound where the station was, nothing remains of it. Recently, the hospital gained fame for being used as a location for a George Clooney film called 'The Jacket' when the former hospital was transformed into an American psychiatric asylum; the only time the public have clamoured to get into the former hospital.

Exploring the Railway Heritage

All the routes in this chapter are covered by the following maps:
Landranger 65; Explorer 343, 349 and 350

Bathgate Upper to Morningside

The Bathgate Upper to Morningside route branched from the Bathgate to Airdrie line at Polkemmet Junction (970680), half a mile south-east of Bathgate Upper Station (now just called Bathgate Station), to reach Whitburn. From there, the railway curved south-west towards Bents and Fauldhouse before continuing south-west to Morningside in Lanarkshire. This North British branch was fourteen miles in length and had stations at Whitburn (2.25 miles from Bathgate Upper), Bents (4.5 miles), and Fauldhouse (6.5 miles).

The trackbed of the branch between Bathgate Upper Station and the M8 is difficult to explore due to building developments blocking it. The section from the site of Whitburn Station, located just south of the A705, to near Bents is a walkway. From Bents to the A706 is difficult but the final section into Fauldhouse has also been turned into a walkway. North of Fauldhouse on the exposed Fauldhouse and Polkemmet moor, the NBR and the CR opened mineral lines to serve the many coal mines. The Bathgate to Fauldhouse section closed in 1964.

Bathgate Station to the M8

The Airdrie and Bathgate Junction Railway was built to exploit the coal and limestone resources between these two towns. The fourteen and a half mile route opened in August 1862 and had stations at Armadale (2.5 miles from Bathgate Upper), Westcraigs (5.25 miles), Forrestfield (8.5 miles), Caldercruix (10 miles), Plains (12 miles), Clarkston (13 miles) and Airdrie (14 miles). There were branches to both Armadale and Woodend Collieries and a link to the Shotts branch from Westcraigs Junction.

Sustrans has opened a cycle route from Bathgate to Drumgelloch Station in Airdrie thus preserving this route almost in its entirety. It is very possible that this route will be re-instated to relieve congestion on the other intercity railway routes. Sculptures provide an interesting addition to the trail and offer a sometimes tenuous link to the railway's industrial past (Fred Flintstone's Bedrock Bike). Access at the Bathgate end is off the B7002 south of the Edgar Allen Railway Engineer's plant, south-east of Bathgate Station. The cycle track climbs and crosses the Bathgate Water. A sculpture called 'Poured Metal' stands beside the bridge, the first of many on this route. Since most of the route is outwith West Lothian, the route is not further explored here.

There was also a branch from the Bathgate Station to the Riddochhill Colliery south of Bathgate. A productive pit, sunk in 1888, it continued to be developed, due to the excellent quality of its coal, well into NCB days until production stopped

Start of the Airdrie to Bathgate walk showing the 'Poured Metal' sculpture

suddenly in 1968 and the M8 motorway was then driven through the site. Water from the pit was used to supply the British Leyland truck plant which lay just to the east of the mine. Part of the former trackbed is used as an off-road cycle track and can also be accessed from the start of the Bathgate to Airdrie cycle route. South of the beginning of the Airdrie cycle route was Polkemmet Junction and the start of the former NBR route to Morningside. North of the M8, it is difficult to explore due to industrial development.

Whitburn Station to Fauldhouse

Whitburn Station (963652) was located just south of the A705 and, latterly, the M8. The construction of this motorway severed the route. The station site is found at the start of the walkway in a cutting between Pretoria Cottages and Redmill Court. The road bridge over the line which carries the A705 is intact. Housing development has changed the land around the former station and removed all evidence of the short mineral lines east to Whitrigg coal mine which closed in 1972. The demise of this pit was accelerated when motorway construction cut the railway link although, for a short time, coal was removed by road. The planting of trees especially to the east of the former trackbed has further disguised the area's coal mining past. The station opened in 1864 in the twilight of EGR days and closed in 1930 when the passenger service of five trains a day with an extra train on Saturdays was withdrawn.

South of the station, the former route, now a tarmac path, begins a long steady climb. The views of Arthur's seat, the 'Five Sisters' shale bings at Westwood outside Livingston and the Pentland Hills are familiar to many. The trackbed emerges from woodlands planted along the route and crosses a minor road where there was once a level crossing. A further network of mineral lines which served the many mines in the Addiewell area such as Loganlea and Stoneyburn and the Addiewell Oil Works branched just south of where the trackbed crosses the Foulshiels Burn. These routes which closed in April 1963 can be traced in part. The NBR and the CR competed for business in this area with the latter providing branches north from their Edinburgh route.

The next station on the line was Bents and, still climbing, the railway entered a cutting on the approach to the station. Conditions underfoot can be difficult and the first possible access via the village and the B7015 is recommended. The station (967622) is located on the minor road north of the main street. The long low

Site of Bents Station
showing lamp hut

stone-built station house beside the line is to the south of what was another level crossing. A traditional corrugated iron lamp hut graces the station house garden. The trackbed emerges from woods to the right.

To avoid private property, follow the B7015 which passes through Bents. The trackbed runs to the west of the road. An attractive woodland walk lies to the east of the road and is a pleasant option. There are views south over the valley towards Leven Seat and the Gladsmuir Hills. In the valley, the ex-Caledonian Glasgow to Edinburgh route runs parallel in this section to the A71. The trackbed then crosses over the B7015 where boarding kennels are located. It is best to follow the road until its junction with the A706 and turn left at the junction to find steps which lead up to the old railway embankment. There was a railway bridge over the A706. To the north, Longridge is situated on the top of a steep hill which explains the route taken by the railway.

From here, there is a walkway along the disused railway as far as Fauldhouse. The trackbed passes under several overbridges with elliptical arches and also past the memorial stone to 10 year old Joseph Townsley who was tragically killed at this spot in September 2003 as the result of a quad bike accident.

Determined to get value from the route, the NBR developed a mineral line to the Leven Seat Quarry to the south. The line crossed the CR line and passed under the A71 before branching into many sidings. Evidence of this line still remains. Fauldhouse and Crofthead Station which lay to the west of Bridge Street in Fauldhouse has been demolished. It consisted of a single storey stone-built station building with a canopy projecting over the single platform. A tiny piece of the platform remains.

Polkemmet Moor

Between the station and the Caledonian line, a mineral line snaked away north-west to start the climb towards Fauldhouse and Polkemmet Moor. This line was in competition with the CR line which branched north-west from their Edinburgh route to reach the moors. The NBR route served the gas works, Braehead East Quarry and Falahill Colliery and ended at Benhar East almost a mile and three quarters from the NBR station. A mining village of over 700 people developed around the East Benhar mine but by 1932, when the mine was not in operation, the council moved the population to nearby Fauldhouse. Living conditions so high on the exposed moor must have been very difficult.

The CR system which left its Edinburgh route at Benhar Junction, west of the Caledonian Fauldhouse Station, served Braehead Quarry and Braehead Colliery before branching to Starryshaw Colliery and sidings at Benhar West and Harthill and Cultrigg Colliery. The Caledonian Station was known as Fauldhouse for Crofthead until 1872 when it was re-named Fauldhouse North. The station is still open and is now called Fauldhouse.

In time, the two railway systems did link up and both railways competed for coal haulage from Greenrigg and Polkemmet mines. The Polkemmet Colliery which was sunk in 1915 but took several years to come into operation, partly due to restrictions imposed by the First World War, lay to the north-west across the moor quite close to Whitburn almost three and a half miles from Fauldhouse. The miners' strike of 1984 led to the mine workings flooding and the pit closed

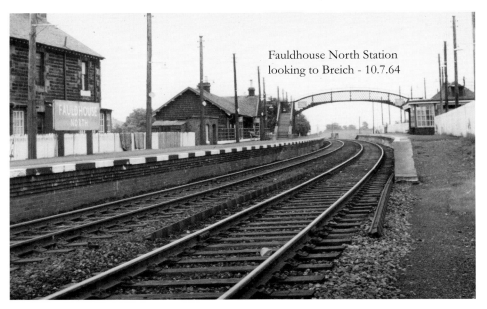

Fauldhouse North Station looking to Breich - 10.7.64

in 1986. The eastern extremity of the Polkemmet Moor is about a mile from the start of the walk at the site of Whitburn Station. The area is covered by a conifer plantation except around the Polkemmet colliery. There are many walks in the area and remnants of the railways and pitheads abound but it can be difficult to identify different sidings and easy to get lost. Some of the ponds are heavily polluted with, amongst other substances, arsenic so care should be taken.

Polkemmet Moor lies to the south of the M8 but travellers along this busy route may not be aware of its industrial past and probably only notice the Harthill

Fauldhouse Station today looking towards Shotts - still the same footbridge

service area and the transmitter masts further west at Kirk O'Shotts. This high and exposed moorland was a difficult and often hostile environment but its black produce was one much sought after.

The railway continued west from Fauldhouse passing under the CR line before reaching the Lanarkshire border. Further west, there was a branch from Blackhill Junction to Shotts, another NBR raid into Caledonian territory which was closed in 1950. The Shotts to Westcraigs Junction line which connected to the Airdrie to Bathgate line survived until 1963. Morningside Station and its surrounding iron works was the final destination for the coal and ironstone mined around Penicuik (described in the chapter 'Railways of the North Esk Valley') and it was initially carted down the steep Kevock bank to be loaded on wagons to start the long railway journey on the short Esk Valley Railway (EVR) in Midlothian to Lanarkshire. The small station made an end-on connection with the Caledonian station in Morningside which was located beside it. Both Morningside stations were closed in 1930.

Bathgate Lower to Blackston and Manuel

The route from Bathgate Lower Station to Blackston Junction (where it joined the MR) was a steady four mile climb with one intermediate station at Westfield (2.75 miles from Bathgate). Nothing remains of Bathgate Lower Station or of the junction site at Blackston. Some of the trackbed has been removed and it is difficult to follow since only short sections remain. Westfield Station (938724) site can be identified where it crosses the B8047 at an angle. The simple wooden platform and shed have been removed but the station cottage and a hut still exist. In sight of the station is the 12 arch Avon Viaduct, a listed structure, built in 1850 to cross the River Avon. The viaduct of rock-faced ashlar has brick facing inside the arches and iron bracing plates at the arch heads. There are two smaller arches at each end of the viaduct. Crumbling concrete beams are found to each side of the trackbed.

The main source of income for the railway was the nearby Westfield Paper Mill which used the water of the River Avon to produce high quality coated papers. It survived for longer than West Lothian's other paper mills but the mill has now closed and the clearance of the site has removed all traces of the railway and the sidings. There was a limited passenger service of two trains daily between Bathgate and Manuel via Blackston but this ceased in 1930.

Twelve arch Avon Viaduct

Branches around Broxburn and Uphall

The Edinburgh to Bathgate line, re-opened in 1986, branches from the intercity line at Newbridge Junction near Ratho, crosses the Union Canal by the eight arch Birdsmill Viaduct, passes to the south of Broxburn and skirts Uphall village. Uphall Station lies immediately south of the village on the other side of the M8 motorway next to Pumpherston Road. The route then continues through Livingston North Station (formerly known as Livingston) before passing under the M8 motorway to reach Bathgate. A completely new station, Livingston South, was opened in 1984 on the old CR line reflecting the increasing size of the new town of Livingston.

A busy mineral line branched from Winchburgh on the Edinburgh and Glasgow route and passed through Broxburn to reach the Bathgate line at Drumshoreland Station (086707) which was known as Broxburn until 1870 and closed in 1951. Another Broxburn Station, this time on the Edinburgh and Glasgow line, was open from 1842 until 1844 and re-opened briefly in 1848. South of Broxburn, traces of the line run parallel to the Union Canal heading north towards the A89 which crosses each of them by bridges. North of the A89, large sections of the trackbed through Broxburn have been built upon and little remains of this once important mineral route until east of the Union Canal and north of West Farm where it linked with the Edinburgh and Glasgow line at Broxburn Junction. West of the canal crossing, the site of the Broxburn Oil Works, world famous for candles amongst other products, has been replaced by an industrial estate.

Mineral lines extended in several directions around the re-opened Uphall Station (061706). One headed east towards Roman Camp and Broxburn before joining up with the mineral line from Winchburgh. Another headed north through Uphall village from the Bathgate line to Ecclesmachan and then veered east towards Winchburgh and its important oil shale works. Only short sections of this line remain and they are found north of Upper Uphall village. A railway walk has been constructed from Uphall Station to East Calder along another former mineral line crossing the impressive Camps Viaduct over the River Almond. The route passes through part of the Almondell Country Park. Whatever direction the railways took, the shale oil and coal industries were the main focus.

The Railway Walk from Uphall to East Calder

The two and a half mile walk crosses the site of the former Pumpherston Oil Works, the last in Scotland to close down in 1964, before reaching the attractive Almondell Country Park. The route is clearly signposted and the trackbed is generally in good condition. South-east from Uphall Station, the former trackbed has been turned into a path. The walk starts beside the former railway line and a modern housing estate before edging out towards Drumshoreland Muir and the Uphall Nature Reserve.

In common with all the mineral lines in the area, the line was once busy and, to most people, a vital link on which many jobs depended. As previously noted, Pumpherston was the centre of the shale oil industry and the moorland is littered with remnants from its past. For those who demand beauty on a walk, the distinctively shaped Binny Craig hill to the north and glimpses of high ground to the south will have to suffice as much of the moor is reclaimed land. Those who once worked here will have difficulty in locating some of the sites of their working past such has been the transformation. The tall brick chimneys belching smoke and the gantries conveying shale and coal have long since disappeared.

Paths lead off the main track in several directions including the start of the line east towards the junction with the Winchburgh branch. Deep ponds are also found close to the trackbed and signs warning of the dangers of subsidence remain. The trackbed winds across the moor passing between two bings before it reaches a road bridge over the line which carries a minor road. On each side are disused workings with major reclamation works to the left. Beyond the bridge are the brick abutments of a dismantled bridge and several buildings. To the left is an embankment leading to the works and to the right are the fairways of Pumpherston Golf Club. Two reed beds catch the water draining from the reclaimed land of the golf course where micro organisms help to break down pollutants. The route then passes poultry farms at the wooded edge of Almondell Country Park. Despite further evidence of old mines, the countryside is more lush as the major engineering feature on this line, the Camps Viaduct built in 1855, is reached. The nine segmental brick arches tower seventy five feet above the River Almond and as well as providing views over the heavily wooded valley, the canal feeder which diverts water from the River Almond to the Union Canal can be seen. Downstream, part of the canal feeder is carried over the river by an aqueduct built in 1820. The cast iron trough on a cantilevered support is an attractive feature. The trackbed reaches East Calder, a few hundred yards beyond the viaduct but this is the end of the railway walk. The country park is well worth a visit since it has an interesting history and a great variety of wildlife. The South car park is located a short distance east from the end of the walk.

The railway passed under the B7015 but from here, the trackbed is very overgrown and difficult to follow. It soon curves east towards the former Raw Camps Mine and Limeworks near Raw Farm. Never a very efficient industry, the oil shale production consumed a large quantity of coal, hence the need for the branch line.

A large and important quarry lay to the east of the B7031 on what is now a poultry farm on part of the Camps Industrial estate. A measure of the importance of this area can be further confirmed by the existence of a CR branch from their Edinburgh to Glasgow main line, east of Kirknewton Station, formerly Midcalder Station, to the quarry and mines near Camps.

Other mineral lines

It is difficult to trace many of the mineral lines which abounded across the West Lothian countryside feeding coal mines, quarries and shale oil pits. Around Philpstoun, little remains of the lines which branched from the Edinburgh to Glasgow railway and crossed the Union Canal to reach the Philpstoun Shale Works (056767) which closed in 1931. There is only a short section of the mineral line to the shale works at Bridgend (037758) which branched further west from the Edinburgh to Glasgow railway.

At Winchburgh, a narrow gauge (2feet 6inch) electric railway transported shale and miners from the Niddry Castle Oil Works to the shale oil works. Around West Calder, there was an extensive network of mineral lines serving various shale pits and coal mines. The CR operated branches north and south of their main line through West Calder. Further east at Midcalder, the waste from the Oakbank Oil Company shale works created an enormous bing. This bing together with others in the area is now undergoing reclamation and landscaping with plants and trees being used to improve the soil and encourage wildlife to return.

Coal and shale was mainly brought in by rail but at Dedridge mine (now part of Livingston new town), an aerial ropeway was used to cover the short distance to the oil works. There were further shale mines at Alderstane and at Deans near Livingston Station. The Westwood works were located close to the 'Five Sisters' shale bings, now a listed monument, which lie to the east of the Freeport Village. The Seafield oil works were to the north of the Westwood works. The story of the oil shale industry is told at the Almond Valley Heritage Centre in Livingston and is worth a visit.

Landscaping and land reclamation combined with the development of Livingston new town and the expansion of private housing and industrial estates have removed most traces of the mineral railways in the area. The most obvious signs of West Lothian's industrial past are the shale bings. These colourful man-made monuments, unique to West Lothian and several of which are now listed industrial monuments, are a permanent reminder of a once proud innovative Scottish industry which led the world for a brief time.

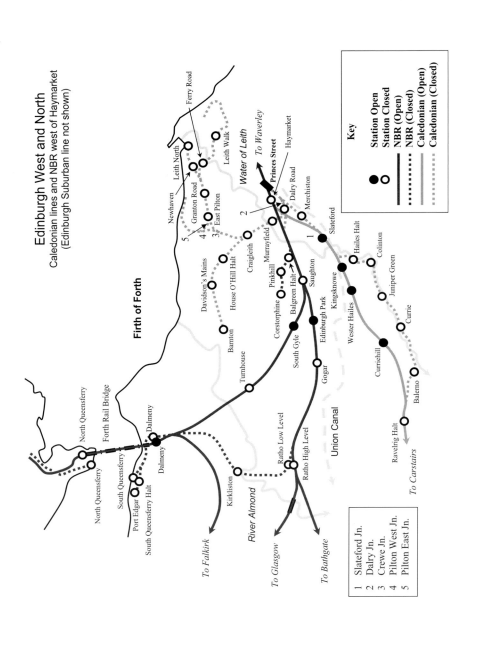

Edinburgh West and North
Caledonian lines and NBR west of Haymarket
(Edinburgh Suburban line not shown)

Firth of Forth

Water of Leith

To Waverley

Union Canal

River Almond

To Falkirk

To Glasgow

To Bathgate

To Carstairs

Ferry Road
Newhaven
Leith North
Granton Road
East Pilton
Leith Walk
Davidson's Mains
House O'Hill Halt
Craigleith
Barnton
Corstorphine
Pinkhill
Murrayfield
Balgreen Halt
Saughton
Edinburgh Park
Turnhouse
South Gyle
Gogar
Slateford
Merchiston
Dalry Road
Princes Street
Haymarket
Kingsknowe
Wester Hailes
Hailes Halt
Colinton
Juniper Green
Currie
Curriehill
Balerno
Ravelrig Halt
North Queensferry
Forth Rail Bridge
South Queensferry
Port Edgar
South Queensferry Halt
North Queensferry
Dalmeny
Dalmeny
Kirkliston
Ratho Low Level
Ratho High Level

Key

●	Station Open
○	Station Closed
▬	NBR (Open)
▪▪▪	NBR (Closed)
▬	Caledonian (Open)
▪▪▪	Caledonian (Closed)

1 Slateford Jn.
2 Dalry Jn.
3 Crewe Jn.
4 Pilton West Jn.
5 Pilton East Jn.

Chapter 6

The Balerno Branch and the Ratho to Queensferry Branch Railways.

Mills, Paper and Everest : the Balerno Branch

This was a railway with all the ingredients to make it live in peoples' memories. It was both an industrial line in rural surroundings with links to the many mills along the banks of the Water of Leith and a passenger line which took people from Edinburgh to the countryside. Operating conditions were demanding as the branch, from the Caledonian Railway (CR) main line into Edinburgh, climbed steadily for five miles from Balerno Junction to Balerno Station through the narrow and twisting valley of the Water of Leith. The severity of the curves and gradients led to locomotives (nick-named 'Balerno Pugs') being specially built for use on the line. A loop was created by extending the line to Ravelrig Junction where it joined up with the CR's main line again further west.

Access to the traffic generated by the twenty-two mills on this section of the Water of Leith was the main attraction for the CR who were anxious to develop business for their Glasgow to Edinburgh main line and expand in the Edinburgh area. The mills produced a variety of products including snuff, grain, meal, spices, woodflour for linoleum and specialist papers for bank notes. Paper mills included Kate's Mill near Colinton, Woodhall near Juniper Green, Balerno Mill and Kinleith Mill which was the largest. The railway carried away the finished paper and brought in the esparto grass, lime and coal required in its manufacture. When excise duty was removed from esparto grass in 1861, it largely replaced rags in the manufacture of paper and this led to increased production and improved quality. Edinburgh Zoo benefited when snakes and spiders caught up in the bales of esparto grass were sent there. The mills sometimes converted to other products. Byrnie Mill near Balerno which originally produced tea and grey paper became a sawmill and Boag Mill switched from paper production to snuff, grain and spice.

The railway also encouraged the development of the many villages in the valley. Juniper Green had already been popular with visitors and in time, the stations provided for the villages of Colinton, Juniper Green, Currie and Balerno helped these communities to expand. The Balerno branch eventually opened in August 1874, nine years after it had been authorised. The initial share capital raised for the branch was spent on other projects due to the financial crisis the CR was experiencing. The company even considered abandoning the line but the local mill owners and the shareholders were not prepared to let this happen and a compromise was eventually reached with the original proposal for a double track line being cut back to single and local landowners accepting less compensation for their land. The new Act required the CR company to deposit the building costs for the branch in a special account and promise to complete construction by December 1872. The Act also provided for the extension of the railway west from Balerno Station to meet the CR's main line at Ravelrig. On the new plans, the extension left the original route a quarter of a mile before the proposed site of Balerno Station. The station was altered and the original site for the station became the goods yard. Between Balerno and Ravelrig Junction, the Ravelrig and Hannahfield Quarries became another source of income with short feeder tramways, mainly horse drawn, being built between the quarries and loading banks beside the railway.

The building of the line involved the construction of many cuttings and embankments, 28 bridges, 4 river crossings and a long tunnel at Colinton and this meant that the December 1872 deadline was not met. The construction of the signal boxes and station cottages, together with the stations and goods sheds at Currie and Balerno did not start until 1873 and the railway eventually opened in August 1874. Stations were built at Colinton, Juniper Green, Currie and Balerno for the opening of the line and in 1908, a platform was built at Hailes primarily for the use of golfers. To the west of Ravelrig Junction, a platform was opened in 1884 on the Caledonian main line but it was not successful until it was upgraded in 1927 for use by golfers travelling to the newly- opened Dalmahoy Golf Course.

Initially there was a service of six trains from Edinburgh terminating at Midcalder with seven in the opposite direction. A turntable eased operations at Midcalder but it was 1899 before a turntable was installed at Balerno. Demand for the passenger service was initially disappointing since most of the locals worked long hours in the mills and had neither the time nor the money to travel. Sunday was their only day off but there was no Sunday service until 1913. Passenger traffic on the line did improve with the increasing popularity of excursions to the foothills of the Pentlands and the development of Colinton and Juniper Green.

As the Second World War approached, passenger services peaked at 21 trains a day but in 1937 the Sunday service was withdrawn and this put the railway at an immediate disadvantage since competition from buses and trams was fierce. The war brought reduced services and in 1943, with just two weeks notice, the passenger service was suspended and never re-instated. In 1956, a new siding was provided for Woodhall paper mill which was now under new ownership but goods traffic eventually declined and with the closure of the Kinleith paper mill in 1966, the branch could no longer be sustained and closed completely in December 1967.

The trackbed of the Balerno Branch has survived as part of the Water of Leith Walkway and its exploration is worthwhile.

Planes, Bridges and Ferries : Ratho to Queensferry

This six and a half mile line branched from the intercity route near Ratho, west of Edinburgh, to Queensferry where a ferry across the Firth of Forth to Fife had been in operation for almost nine hundred years. Queensferry got its name for being precisely that: it carried Queen Margaret, wife of the Scottish King Malcolm Canmore across the Forth from Edinburgh to their favourite retreat in Dunfermline. The branch was opened in 1868 to take advantage of this ancient crossing and it was extended through South Queensferry to Port Edgar in 1878 to develop passenger business further.

Today, much has changed around the route of the railway with the trackbed now overlooked by Edinburgh Airport and the Forth road and railway bridges. When the railway bridge opened, the passenger service came to an end although it was revived in 1919 for ten years. During the bridge's construction to provide the missing link in quick rail travel to the north, two new approach routes were built on the south bank of the Forth which accelerated the demise of the Ratho branch. Both routes branched from the Edinburgh and Glasgow intercity route. From Saughton Junction near Corstorphine Hill, a five and a quarter mile branch was built to Dalmeny South Junction - a quicker route for those travelling west from Edinburgh to the bridge. Near Winchburgh, a four and a half mile branch was built to Dalmeny North Junction on the Ratho branch, making it easier for traffic from the west to reach the bridge. From Dalmeny North Junction, the final approaches to the Forth Rail Bridge were built along with a new station at Dalmeny.

Exploring the Railway Heritage

All the routes in this chapter are covered by the following maps: Landranger 65 and 66; Explorer 349 and 350.

The Balerno Branch

The route can be walked from near Balerno Junction to Balerno Station. The enthusiast can continue to Ravelrig Junction although this latter part is not so easy. There were stations at Colinton (1.5 miles from Balerno Junction), Juniper Green (2.5 miles), Currie (3.75 miles) and Balerno (5 miles). The Colinton tunnel is still open.

For added interest, the walk can start with a visit to the Water of Leith Visitor Centre (24 Lanark Road), a short distance east along the Lanark Road (A70), where the Balerno branch started. The exhibitions highlight the historical and continuing importance of the Water of Leith to the area. Rising from the Colzium springs and travelling almost 24 miles to the port of Leith, the river was arguably one of the most productive in Scotland with no less than 76 water-powered mills along its length. It was the power house for the manufacturing industry in and around Edinburgh. To ensure continuity of water supply to the city, the Harlaw and Threipmuir Reservoirs were built in the 1800s to the south of Balerno in the Pentland Hills.

From the visitor centre, steps climb to the Union Canal and the impressive eight-arched Slateford Aqueduct which was built with stone from the nearby Redhall Quarry and is lined with an iron trough. It runs parallel to the fourteen-arch Slateford Railway Viaduct which carries the former CR line over the Water of Leith. Along the canal towpath, a high arched footbridge over the Lanark Road is reached by crossing the former railway bridge, the first on the Balerno branch, which has now been converted to a footbridge over the canal. In the bushes to the right is the site of Balerno Junction (216704) where the branch joined the former CR route. The journey along the former railway route begins on the far side of the footbridge. The walk along the valley of the Water of Leith changes from winter to summer. In summer, the extensive foliage restricts views which in winter are more extensive. The tranquil, mostly tree lined route is very attractive compared to the busy A70 and must be totally changed from what it was like when the mills were in operation.

The trackbed first passes under a road bridge (Redhall Bank Road), originally part of the A70, before quarrying meant the road was shifted north. It continues over the access road to Boag's (Bog's Mill) which once made paper for the Bank of Scotland but when the railway came, it was a snuff, grain and spice mill. It burnt down in 1924 and the site is now occupied by a private house. Millbank House to the right of the line was where the Directors of the bank supposedly waited while the paper for their notes was being produced. Across the river valley is Redhall House. The trackbed now enters Colinton Dell. Even this early, a pattern had been set where mills were found clinging to the narrow valley side, some even built jutting out over the river, to trap the energy of the Water of Leith. In this cramped, almost claustrophobic setting, the river was used to generate power for all types of mills. The sides of the valley were often too steep to make it easy to bring goods in and out by road and the railway offered an outlet for the products of the many mills.

As the track turns south-west, a path diverges from the trackbed which once led to Kate's paper mill (closed 1890). The sidings are very overgrown. A short distance further on was Hailes Halt, opened in November 1908 to cater for the increasing popularity of golf. Courses nearer to Edinburgh were becoming too busy and the arrival of the railway encouraged the development of several golf courses along its length. Torphin Hill Golf Course near Juniper Green Station was opened in 1903 and in 1907 a new course was constructed at Kingsknowe with the club house very close to the Lanark Road. The platform at Hailes was only a short climb to the golf course to the north of the Lanark Road. The CR company was initially lukewarm but after being guaranteed an annual income, a platform was built. Passengers intending to use the platform had to inform station staff in advance before boarding the train at other stations en route. Nothing remains of the platform.

Hailes Platform looking to Edinburgh

A weir was built to serve Redhall and Kate's mills and can be seen from the trackbed to the right where a retaining wall was built after a landslip. The former railway is carved out of the hillside and this continues until the start of the curved 149 yard Colinton tunnel. Still open and lit, the brick lined tunnel with a painting of a Caley locomotive towards the exit on the left hand side emerges on to the site of Colinton Station (214691) which was to the right of the line. A cairn erected to mark the opening of the old route as a walkway, indicates where the station was located beside the tunnel mouth. The station building was modest with a short canopy and a long wooden fence separated the passengers from the goods yard behind. Ahead is the eight-arched bridge (B701) built at the same time as the railway and subsequently widened. A wooden goods shed at an angle to the line dominated the station and was accessed through the last two arches to the right from sidings which started beyond the bridge. A selection of mill stones is found at the bridge maintaining a connection with many mills along the route.

Colinton Station - 5.7.58

The trackbed continues past Spylaw House once the home of James Gillespie, a tobacco and snuff manufacturer, who funded many projects including James Gillespie School in Edinburgh. After passing Spylaw Park, the site of the former Scott's Porage Oats Factory is reached. This is now occupied by offices and flats. Some of the mill buildings were built over the sidings so that goods wagons emerged through them to reach the branch line. Nearly a third of the wagons dispatched from the sidings only went as far as Colinton Station - a very short journey!

At this point, the railway crosses the river for the first time and follows the south bank for a short distance until it is forced to cross the river again. More mill conversions and weirs are passed but ahead is a new bridge which carries the City of Edinburgh by-pass - a loud intrusion into the quiet peace of the Dell. On the far side, new constructions on the site of Woodhall Mill force a well-signposted detour. This mill closed in 1984, its final product being board for the whisky industry.

Cairn at the site of Colinton Station

The former railway now approaches Juniper Green Station (198685) which was located where the dispatch shed for Woodhall Mill stands. This is now used as a bathroom showroom. A winding path up the hillside to St Margaret's Church, a notable landmark on the Lanark Road, can still be traced from behind a bench beside the trackbed. The station was similar in style to Colinton but positioned on an acute curve. The other paper and snuff mills in the vicinity of the station have been demolished.

The railway crosses the river again and passes under the road bridge to Blinkbonny before reaching the site of the Kinleith Mill which was once the fifth largest paper mill in the country and the biggest by far in the valley. The mill latterly produced featherweight book papers but closed in 1966 at which time the site became an industrial estate before being recently cleared. Still climbing, the railway trackbed approaches Currie and passes the manse, the old school and Currie Kirk before crossing over Kirkgate. The station at Currie (182675) was located between the railway bridge and the goods sidings. The goods shed at the end of the siding behind the station is still intact but little else remains.

At last, the trackbed reaches more open countryside with views towards the Pentland Hills. Retaining walls were still required beside the track and on these walls, Dougal Haston, the famous Everest climber, first practised his handholds and climbing techniques.

There is a fourth and final crossing of the river before Balerno is reached. Today, the Water of Leith Walkway ends on Bridge Road beside Balerno High School where the goods yard was located. The final section towards the station passes under the A70 and enters a cutting where the station was located (164671). Today, the site is under construction and is a private road. Beyond the station, the route continues to Ravelrig Junction where it rejoins the former CR route into Edinburgh.

Ratho Station to Port Edgar

The route is intact north of the A8 through Ratho Station, to the supermarket in Queensferry east of the B907. Beyond this point, detours are required and conditions deteriorate. There were stations at Ratho Low Level Platform (132724), Kirkliston (127733), Dalmeny (140779), South Queensferry (133782) and Port Edgar (119792).

Ratho Station is about half a mile north of the attractive village of Ratho. The Union Canal runs along the north side of the village and offers canal trips. The canal follows the 240 foot contour but the railway ran further to the north, separated by a hill from the canal. Ratho Station, therefore, developed as a separate village. The main line station (132723) sometimes known as Ratho High Level was located beside Station Road where the road crossed over the main line. One of the crumbling platforms can still be seen beside the rails. The road bridge is now closed to vehicles.

Queensferry Junction (135722) where the Queensferry line branched, lay slightly to the east of the main line Ratho High Level Station. Ratho Low Level Station (132724) was located at the start of the Queensferry branch, between the junction and the High Level Station. The platforms of the station on the Queensferry line remain. Ratho Station Industrial Estate occupies most of the area between the station sites and the A8 and there are no further traces of the railway until north of that road.

The line then turned north towards Newbridge. Today, this section has been transformed as the M8 and M9 meet at a busy interchange to the west of Ratho Station. The A8 Glasgow Road heads east towards Edinburgh from the road interchange passing through Ratho Station and south of the Royal Highland Showground and Edinburgh Airport before reaching the outskirts of Edinburgh. The railway once passed under the road. From a footbridge over the busy A8, all the familiar Edinburgh landmarks can be seen with Edinburgh Airport prominent and over high ground to the north, the familiar twin bridges over the Forth. Not often in railway journeys can you so clearly see the end from the beginning.

Having crossed the footbridge, turn left and continue until the roundabout is reached. The trackbed is beside the start of the M9. It is very straight and starts to climb on an embankment. Beyond the first railway bridge where there is a sewage works, a mineral line once extended north-east over a minor road to a coal pit near Lennie Mains. There is no trace of this route, most of which now lies inside the perimeter fence of Edinburgh Airport.

Near Hallyards is a skewed, arched overbridge (bridge number 4). The trackbed continues to climb with views of Kirkliston village and the attractive church tower (now the Thomas Chalmers Centre). The four-arched, sandstone-faced viaduct over the Almond River is crossed before the village is reached. Prominent, although likely to be demolished shortly, is Kirkliston Distillery, one of the original grain distilleries, which formed part of the Distillers Company Limited. Although mainly a grain distillery, it did experiment with malt but closed early last century. DCL used it to make yeast and the high red brick building which can still be seen, was added in the 1930s. Railway sidings extended to the distillery which for a while was used to make kits for home brewing.

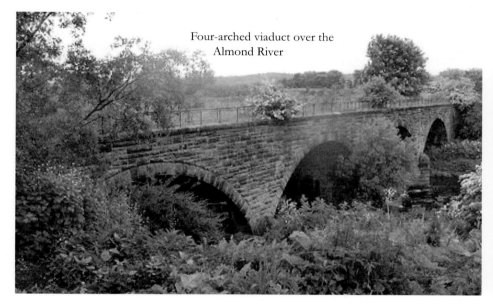

Four-arched viaduct over the
Almond River

Kirkliston Station building (127733), now demolished, was a low red brick building with a hipped slate roof. The trackbed continued past the station cottage and several other houses before reaching the next overbridge. Beyond it, to the left, is a pipe outlet covered by a metal grille which allowed water to tumble down stone steps to the drainage beside the trackbed. This may have been the outlet pipe from the distillery who paid a fee to the railway each year so that their outflow could run beside the railway to be eventually discharged into the Forth, thus providing an unusual source of income for the railway and saving the distillery a lot of expense.

Still climbing, the trackbed crosses over a road near Carlowrie Cottages by a bridge which is listed category C. Near the summit, the trackbed enters a cutting and reaches a siding that served a naval stores depot which stored uniforms, amongst other items. The siding is still barred with warning signs on the fences but the warehouses are now used by local companies. There was another siding on the east side of the stores which branched from the Winchburgh to Dalmeny line. The trackbed runs parallel to a minor road and reaches the former junction (Dalmeny South). To the right is a major oil depot, partly camouflaged, with an entrance tunnel into the hillside. A path, to the left, just before the junction of the Ratho line with the line from Edinburgh, leaves the trackbed and leads down to a disused road. This disused road becomes a path which winds round what is now a caravan storage park and runs beside the Edinburgh railway. To the left, the Winchburgh line can be seen and ahead, beyond the overbridge which carries the A90, is Dalmeny North Junction. From the junction, the track approaches the present Dalmeny Station before reaching the Forth Railway Bridge. The cantilever sections of the bridge jut above the horizon.

The Ratho to Queensferry trackbed runs to the right of the present railway and heads down into a deep cutting, curving to pass under the bridge. The original Dalmeny Station (140779) was located at an overbridge whose height has been reduced. No trace of the station or goods yard remains. Views towards the railway bridge are restricted at this point due to the wooded hillside. Between Dalmeny Station and South Queensferry halt was a very early halt known as Hall's Platform. The walkway ends at a supermarket. There is no trace of South Queensferry Halt (133782) but an embankment wall overlooking the supermarket is listed and was part of the railway. Sidings near here served the VAT 69 whisky bond.

Climbing up steps from the supermarket and continuing west to a further set of steps, leads to a railway arch which has been half bricked off. The new brick wall is the end of a housing development. From here, the trackbed passes through a wooded area to reach Port Edgar where there was a station on the pier from 1878 until 1890. The conditions underfoot and the rubbish strewn about make this an unattractive option. Overhead looms the Forth Road Bridge. Port Edgar was an important base for mine sweepers and escort craft during the Second World War.

It is appropriate that the last disused branch explored ends underneath one of the most famous railway bridges in the world. The bridge provides an enduring symbol that the finest engineering will survive and that railways have a future. The closure of this branch was directly linked to the building of the railway bridge: a better, more direct route replaced a less useful one. Progress always creates casualties and many of the disused railways described, ceased to serve a useful function. Just as the canals were superseded by the railways, road traffic has taken over as the main means of transport. Like many of the lost railways described, this route has found an alternative use as a walkway which provides an interesting link with the recent social and industrial history of the area. Explore the railway heritage and learn about the past.

Above: bomb damage - Junction Bridge Station, 1941 (Known as Junction Road Station until 1923). See Chapter 4, page 99.

Below: Frontage of North Leith Station. See Chapter 4 (NBR, Leith Citadel)

Further Reading

In preparing the manuscript the author consulted the following books:

John Baldwin, *Edinburgh, Lothians And Borders,* The Stationery Office

Gordon Biddle & O. S. Nock, *Railway Heritage of Britain,*
Studio Editions, 1990

Campbell Brown and Steven Wiggins, *Edinburgh Walks: Volume Two,*
B+W Publishing, 1990

R.V. J. Butt, *Directory of Railway Stations,* Patrick Stephens Ltd, 1995

Mark Collard, *Lothian: A Historical Guide,* Birlinn, 1998

M.H. Ellison, *Scottish Railway Walks,* Cicerone Press Guide, 1989

Ian Finlay, *Lothians,* Collins, 1960

C. J. Gammell, *Scottish Branch Lines,* Oxford Publishing Co. 1999

Andrew M. Hajducki, *Haddington, Macmerry and Gifford branch Lines,*
The Oakwood Press, 1994

Andrew M. Hajducki, *North Berwick and Gullane Branch Lines,*
The Oakwood Press, 1992

William F. Hendrie, *Discovering West Lothian,* John Donald, 1986

John R. Hume, *Industrial Archaeology of Scotland, 1 The Lowlands and
Borders,* B.T. Batsford Ltd, 1976

D. L. G. Hunter, *Edinburgh's Transport: The Early Years,*
The Mercat Press, 1992

Jeff Hurst, *Glencorse Branch,* The Oakwood Press, 1999

Guthrie Hutton, *Mining The Lothians,* Stenlake Publishing Limited, 1998

Gavin Morrison, *Scottish Railways - Then & Now,* Ian Allan Publishing, 1999

A. J. Mullay, *Rail Centres Number 15: Edinburgh.* Ian Allan Limited, 1991

Robert Robotham, *Waverley Route - The Postwar Years,* Ian Allan
Publishing, 1999

Keith Sanders and Douglas Hodgins, *British Railways, Past and Present,
South East Scotland,* Silver Link Publishing Ltd, 1991

Donald Shaw, *Balerno Branch and the Caley in Edinburgh,* The Oakwood
Press, 1989

Roger Siviter, *Waverley - Portrait of a Famous Route,* Kingfisher Railway
Publications, 1988

Martin Smith, *British Railways Bridges & Viaducts,* Ian Allan Publishing

W. A. C. Smith & Paul Anderson, *Illustrated History of Edinburgh's
Railways,* Irwell Press, 1995

Gordon Stansfield, *Lost Railways of the Scottish Borders,* Stenlake
   Publishing, 1999
John Thomas, *Forgotten Railways Scotland,* David & Charles, 1976
John Thomas,*North British Railway Volume 1,* David and Charles, 1969
John Thomas, *Regional History of the Railways of Great Britain, Scotland:
   The Lowlands and the Borders.* David & Charles, 1984
Joyce M. Wallace, *Canonmills and Inverleith,* John Donald, 1994
Nigel Welbourn, *Lost Lines, Scotland.* Ian Allan Publishing, 1994
West Lothian History and Amenity Society, *Routes Across West Lothian,*
Alasdair Wham, *Border Railway Rambles,* Stenlake Publishing Limited, 2004
Alasdair Wham, *Lost Railway Lines South of Glasgow,* G.C. Book
   Publishers Ltd, 2000
Ian Whyte, *Edinburgh & The Borders - Landscape Heritage,*
   David & Charles

Princes Street Station - 19.4.65 (see Chapter 4 under
Caledonian Railway Branches)

Useful Contacts and Websites

Caledonian Railway Association: www.crassoc.org.uk
Ewan Crawford's Scottish Railway Website: www.railscot.co.uk
G C Books Ltd, Unit 10, Bladnoch Bridge Estate, Wigtown, DG8 9AB;
  www.gcbooks.co.uk
North British Railway Study Group: www.noble101.freeserve.co.uk
Railway Ramblers, Scottish Branch:
  Tony Jervis, 7 Dymond Grove, Dunfermline, KY11 8DE;
  www.railwayramblers.org.uk
Scottish Railway Preservation Society, Bo'ness Station, Union Sttreet, West
  Lothian, EH51 9AQ; www.srps.org.uk
SPOKES (Lothian Cycle Group), St Martin's Church, 232 Dalry Road,
  Edinburgh, EH11 2JG; www.spokes.org.uk
SUSTRANS: Scottish Office, 162 Fountainbridge, Edinburgh, EH3 9RX;
  www.sustrans.org.uk
Water of Leith Conservation Trust, 24 Lanark Road, Edinburgh, EH14 1TQ;
  www.waterofleith.edin.org
Waverley Railway Project: www.waverleyrailwayproject.co.uk
Waverley Route Heritage Association, Signal Box Cottage, Whitrope,
  Hawick, TD9 9TY; www.wrha.org.uk

End of the line - near South Queensferry